White Vulcan at take off, making a steep climb.

MY TARGET WAS
LENINGRAD

V FORCE: PRESERVING OUR DEMOCRACY

PHILIP GOODALL

FONTHILL

Fonthill Media Language Policy

Fonthill Media publishes in the international English language market. One language edition is published worldwide. As there are minor differences in spelling and presentation, especially with regard to American English and British English, a policy is necessary to define which form of English to use. The Fonthill Policy is to use the form of English native to the author. Philip Goodall was born and educated in England and now lives in Northamptonshire and therefore British English has been adopted in this publication.

Fonthill Media Limited
Fonthill Media LLC
www.fonthillmedia.com
office@fonthillmedia.com

First published in the United Kingdom
and the United States of America 2015

British Library Cataloguing in Publication Data:
A catalogue record for this book is available from the British Library

Typeset in Sabon LT Std 10/13.5
Printed and bound by CPI Group (UK) Ltd, Croydon, CR0 4YY

Contents

Acknowledgements

I'd like to express my gratitude to Peter G. Dancey and Alexander Mladenov for their contributions to this book. Peter for lending his expertise in the writing of the separate section on the Avro Vulcan, and Alexander for writing the sections on the Soviet Su-9, MiG-21, and Tu-128 fighters, and the Tu-95 bomber, and for providing photographs for the latter three.

PJG's Valiant crew with Flight Lieutenants Warwick, Rumbol, Hunt, and Master Signalman Allen.

PROLOGUE

A Changing World

On 29 March 1945, when the war in Europe was coming to an end, Air Chief Marshal Sir Arthur Harris wrote to the Deputy Chief of the Air Staff pondering what would happen in the war against Japan, where an invasion could cost between 3 and 6 million casualties. I note that in 2012 a number of Spitfires were found in Burma which presumably had been sent by sea in preparation for the war against Japan. In the summer of 1945, Group Captain G. L. Cheshire VC and Dr W. Penney were sent to join the USAAF on Tinian Island in the Pacific. On 6 August 1945, three B-29s flew from Tinian Island to Hiroshima, one to drop the bomb, the second to make scientific observations, and the third to photograph the explosion. On 9 August, three aircraft flew to Nagasaki with the same responsibilities as those that had bombed Hiroshima. Group Captain Cheshire and Dr W. Penney witnessed both bombings from the aircraft photographing the attack. Japan surrendered on 10 August 1945. The means of fighting a major war had changed.

The world was also changing in the UK with a general election on 5 July 1945, which brought the Labour Party into power. The new Prime Minister, Clement Attlee, set up an Advisory Committee on Atomic Energy. On 29 August he circulated a memorandum on the atomic bomb:

A decision on major policy with regard to the atomic bomb is imperative. Until this is taken, civil and military departments are unable to plan. It must be recognised that the emergence of this weapon has rendered most of our post-war planning out of date.

There were numerous political, military, and scientific discussions regarding the research and the production of nuclear weapons and their means of delivery against a potential enemy. It was decided to establish a nuclear research establishment at Hartwell, in part because the United States stated that they would not share with the UK the secrets of the production of nuclear weapons. An analysis of the RAF nuclear capability and a chronology of the political, military, and international events are included in the Appendix.

Above: Crew running towards their Vulcan Mk2.

Opposite: On 12 April 1967, Philip Goodall had his final handling test at the Vulcan Operational Conversion Unit at RAF Finningley in Yorkshire. He flew Vulcan 558, which is the one remaining Vulcan that is still flying in 2015.

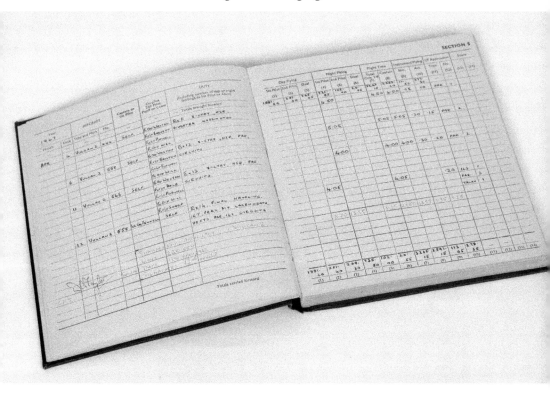

When the war ended in 1945, there were two scientific developments which changed the military strategies of many countries, namely the jet engine and the atomic bomb. It is interesting that the two main political parties in the UK were in general agreement regarding the developments of jet aircraft and nuclear weapons.

In January 1947 the government made the decision to develop the atomic bomb. This was followed by the agreement to develop jet engine aircraft with a range of 2,000 miles with the capability of dropping nuclear weapons and conventional bombs. There was much discussion regarding the crew and means of escape but eventually it was agreed to have a crew of five—two pilots, a navigator radar, navigator plotter, and an air electronics officer who would control the defensive radars. The pilots would have ejection seats and the rear crew the means of a parachute escape. The aircraft would have four jet engines. Four manufacturers submitted plans—Short, Vickers, Avro, and Handley Page. It was decided to order the Valiant from Vickers, the Vulcan from Avro, and the Victor from Handley Page.

Flight Lieutenant Goodall when a Valiant Captain.

I

My Early Life

I was born in the village of Ashburton in Devon which is roughly halfway between Plymouth and Exeter. My mother, the daughter of a local businessman, was born there too—she benefited from a good education at a boarding school and then at a finishing school in Belgium to learn French. My father moved into Ashburton as the senior master at Ashburton Grammar School and met the lady who was to become my mother. They married and sometime later, in June 1930, I was born. My parents had full lives with leading roles in the successful Ashburton Dramatic Society and in sports activities at the school and in the local area.

One evening my parents were invited out to dinner with friends and on their return my father felt unwell. They called the local doctor who said my father had eaten something which had upset him. A couple of days later the doctor returned and realised that my father was suffering from appendicitis, so he was admitted to the local hospital. Two days later, on the morning of 5 November 1938, I visited the hospital and screamed when I saw the yellow-skinned man who was my father. He died from peritonitis later that day. Coincidentally, returning to London on a train after the funeral, my uncles met the surgeon who had carried out the operation. He agreed with them that my father's death was the result of errors committed by the local doctor.

As the wife of a schoolmaster my mother had not been working, and thus had to sell her house when my father, the family breadwinner, died. She moved up to Bournemouth to live with her parents. Five months later, my great aunt, a spinster called Florence Honywill, also died. She had changed her will shortly before her death, making me, a fatherless child of eight, a major beneficiary. She made my father's elder brother the executor, entrusting my father's family with my education. I was told that at her funeral, all her nieces cancelled their wreaths as they had found themselves cut out of her will.

Having been appointed the executor, my uncle, George Goodall, decided that I should go off to boarding school, so from the age of nine to eighteen I had the privilege of a good education. He had two sons and a daughter of his own, yet he found the time to make sure I received the full benefit of my inheritance. I know little of the life of my great aunt, but it is interesting that a spinster lady decided that she would ensure a good education for a young boy. It so happens that my father and my great aunt are buried a few feet apart in the graveyard of Ashburton church. When I visit Ashburton, I stand at the end of her grave and say, 'Thank you.' Sadly my uncle also died before I had the opportunity to express my sincere thanks. I am pleased that my cousins inherited their father's charm and intelligence.

The first school I attended was Crediton Grammar School near Exeter, where the headmaster was apparently a friend of my father. One night we were all woken up and taken underground because the Luftwaffe was bombing Exeter; we wondered why a country city like Exeter should be on the German target list. The extensive destruction of the city centre was horrific.

My uncle decided that I should change schools and in 1942 I moved to Eltham College, but as Eltham is in South East London, all the boarders had been evacuated to Taunton School in Somerset. We remained at Taunton until the end of the war and then went back to Eltham in September 1945. One year we went on a holiday to Switzerland and the press featured the visit of the boys from Eltham College. The school was originally established as the school for the sons of missionaries, but the press got one of their facts wrong and publicised the visit from the school for the sons of millionaires—I guess that missionaries and millionaires do not have too much in common. I spent three years at Eltham and left in the summer of 1948 and with a university scholarship.

2

National Service

In the summer of 1940 I was living in Bournemouth and I remember watching German aircraft being intercepted by RAF fighters. My cousin and I were on the top floor looking out of sky lights on either side of the house. I called him and said that a Spitfire was on fire—the pilot had bailed out but his parachute had not opened. I recall my older cousin shouting at the pilot, 'Pull your ripcord!' but sadly he hit the ground about half a mile from our home. The following day a Messerschmitt 109 was shot down and the pilot bailed out about a mile from the coast.

On 1 January 1949 the National Service Act was implemented and all men aged between seventeen and twenty-one had to do eighteen months' national service, which meant serving in the Army, Navy, or Royal Air Force. With my personal memories of the war—watching fighter pilots over Bournemouth—I had every wish to serve in the RAF. Having left school in 1948 with a higher school certificate and a scholarship to university, I was keen to start my service; I was enrolled into the RAF on 3 March 1949 and my address was Hut 101, 2 Flight, A Squadron, 1 Wing, RAF Padgate, Near Warrington, Lancashire.

I believe there were ninety-six boys in the intake, of which two had attended a public school. We were equipped with our uniforms and bed linen, and started our eight weeks of basic training, learning to march and do as we were told. One day I was instructed to scrub the wooden floor in the office. I had never scrubbed a floor, so I presumed you got a bucket full of water, a scrubbing brush, and off you went. When I had finished it looked fine. The next morning the sergeant threatened to put me on a charge for the total mess of the floor in his office. I explained that it was the first time I'd scrubbed a floor and was rewarded with ample practice. I scrubbed his floor every day for the next week—the secret, I discovered, was to use minimal water so that the floor dries without leaving a filthy watermark.

We all had to take our turn in guarding the camp. I recall being on duty at the main entrance with a rifle and bayonet. As the station was to have its annual inspection, a van arrived with attractive trees and bushes and transformed the banks alongside the entrance into the camp. Apparently the agreement was that the camp would lease the trees to give the right impression to those inspecting, and then return everything to the garden centre. It was a lesson well learnt.

When I think about those days I realise how totally different life is in the UK in the twenty-first century. All of the boys in my group were white, as would be expected in the late 1940s. We accepted our responsibility to serve our country by completing eighteen months' military service. Having lived through the war I suppose it is not surprising that none of our group was overweight. Of course in those days we were financially rewarded—4 shillings a day—but we could not afford to get drunk and I have no recollection of rough or rude behaviour.

After eight weeks we completed our basic training and were sent home for a week before reporting to our next training centre. A telegram arrived instructing me to report to the RAF School of Education, based at RAF Wellesbourne Mountford, just south of Stratford on Avon in Warwickshire. Eight national servicemen arrived, of whom most had attended a teacher's training college. We were informed that we were on a six-week course and would each leave as an Aircraftman 2nd Class (AC2) with the acting rank of sergeant in the Education Branch. Apparently education was mandatory for

Sergeant Goodall doing his
National Service in 1950.

all national servicemen, and I spent the next year teaching my contemporaries. I also have memories of attending the Royal Shakespeare Memorial Theatre in my AC2 uniform, but how we got to Stratford or could afford the tickets escapes me.

I recently revisited Wellesbourne Mountford to bring back a few memories and was most surprised to see Vulcan XM655 at the main entrance. Apparently the Vulcan was delivered to Wellesbourne in 1984 and now has a team of supporters who maintain the aircraft. Occasionally it is taken to the runway and does a 'pretend take-off' with thousands of spectators. I guess the Vulcan remains a unique aircraft in the history of British aviation.

In June 1949 I was posted to RAF Yeadon between Leeds and Harrogate in Yorkshire, better known today as Leeds Bradford Airport. At that time the station was in Reserve Command, which was the organisation responsible for the auxiliary squadrons—squadrons with part-time officers and airmen who worked three weekends a month in the RAF while continuing their main profession, which could be anything from a bank manager to a car mechanic. A study of the Battle of Britain will show that the auxiliary squadrons played an important role as they provided a well-trained force to fight the enemy. No. 609 Squadron was formed in 1936 and was the first squadron credited with reaching 100 and 200 enemy aircraft kills. When I arrived at Yeadon, No. 609 Auxiliary Squadron was still flying the Spitfire. To accommodate the requirements of the auxiliaries, we worked three weekends a month and had a break on the Tuesday and Wednesday.

I arrived at the Sergeants' Mess an eighteen-year-old ex-public schoolboy, where the youngest sergeant was twenty-seven. As you can guess I was not the most popular person in the mess. As it was June I thought it a good idea to play for the station cricket team; to my surprise they had all the training facilities and I was able to demonstrate my abilities. I was told that I had been selected to play but would be the last man in. I explained that I was more of a batsman than a bowler. 'No, we are not talking about the cricket team,' came the reply. 'During every match a young lady comes up from the village and goes into the air-raid shelter and you will be the last man "in"!' An excitement I did not experience.

I learned very quickly with a whole variety of responsibilities, including working at the headquarters that controlled all the stations. Every month in the Sergeants' Mess, a different NCO would have the task of running the bar. On the 1st of the month you would accept financial responsibility for all the stock the bar, which would include spirits, wine, beer, cigarettes, crisps, and all the incidentals. At the end of the month you hoped you would hand over to your successor without incurring a massive debt. It was explained to me that the only way to avoid this debt was to run the bar at a modest profit, and fortunately it worked.

I became friendly with another young man fulfilling his national service duties. He was planning on going off to art college. None of us had any money so I asked my mother to lend me cash for oil paint so my friend could paint my portrait. The artist was Leo Baxendale, who became famous as the creator of the *Beano*, a children's comic. I was very pleased with his painting and it hangs in my lounge to this day. I often wonder if he ever painted anything similar to my portrait.

One morning I was told to report to the station commander. 'Would you like a commission in the Education Branch?' was the question when I arrived. I explained that I was only interested in remaining in the RAF as a pilot. My commanding officer examined the rules and discovered that I was eligible to attend the RAF College, so he immediately sent off the appropriate papers. A short while later I was to go to the Aircrew Selection Centre at RAF Hornchurch, an old Battle of Britain base. I spent a week being examined to see if I could think, see, and hear as demanded. The intelligence tests and related examinations were extensive, which is not surprising considering the financial costs of training a pilot are equivalent to the tuition costs of about 100 university students. I then spent a week at Ramridge House where a team of officers challenged me to lead a group across a river, explain my political views, enter into debates, and explain why I wished to be a pilot. It was a most interesting week; I was in the fortunate position of having a scholarship to university, meaning the fear of failure was not as great for me as it might have been. I was most impressed with the selection procedures which indicated that the RAF spent a great deal of time and money to recruit the most able cadets.

A while after returning to my base, I received a call from the station adjutant to report immediately to the station commander in 'best blue'. I entered his office and saluted. He was sitting at his desk with his hat on and his deputy was standing alongside, also with his hat on, and I wondered what I had done to deserve such a formal welcome. He had a paper on the desk and he read, 'I am commanded by the Air Council to inform you that you have been awarded a cadetship as a pilot in the General Duties Branch of the Royal Air Force.' He then leapt up and congratulated me. My life suddenly changed; I was no longer going to university, but the RAF College at Cranwell.

The other sergeants on the base soon learnt that I was going off to be trained as a pilot and the support and goodwill was quite wonderful. The senior NCO on a base is normally the station warrant officer, and he called me into his office. 'Now, young man, you are going to make a success of your training at Cranwell and I have lots of good advice. The first thing you must do is get another girlfriend, as your young lady is most unsuitable for a young officer.' For the remainder of my time at Yeadon he offered the most wonderful advice as if I was his son; it reflected the camaraderie within the RAF, which I believe is very different to that of the other services.

3

RAF College, Cranwell

In September 1950 I was posted to the RAF College at Cranwell to be trained as a pilot, but at the time I knew nothing about the background and history of the college. In 1915 the Royal Naval Air Service (RNAS) wanted to establish a training unit where officers and ratings could be trained to fly aeroplanes and airships; 2,500 acres from the Earl of Bristol's estate were requisitioned, and on 1 April 1916, The Royal Naval Air Service Central Training Establishment, known as HMS *Daedalus*, was formed at Cranwell. With the amalgamation of the RNAS and the Royal Flying Corps (RFC) on 1 April 1918, Cranwell became Royal Air Force Station Cranwell. After the First World War, Sir Hugh Trenchard was the first Chief of the Air Staff, and he was determined to establish a cadet college to provide flying training for the future leaders of the RAF. He chose Cranwell for very particular reasons:

> [...] marooned in the wilderness, cut off from pastimes they could not organise for themselves, the cadets would find life cheaper, healthier and more wholesome.

The Royal Air Force College was opened on 5 February 1920 and was the first military air academy in the world. It initially consisted of open fields and naval huts, but plans were afoot to construct a substantial college building. During the 1920s there was much discussion about its layout, but the architect James West finally settled on a neo-classical design in the style of the Royal Hospital in Chelsea. College Hall, as it was known, was officially opened by HRH the Prince of Wales, later King Edward VIII, in October 1934.

The building had three wings—'A' Squadron, 'B' Squadron, and 'C' Squadron—and each had the task of training pilots. In 1947 a 'D' Squadron was formed to train secretarial and equipment officers, but it was not based at Cranwell. As with most schools and universities, the college had three terms a year, but unlike other educational establishments, cadets spent eight terms at the college. Every four months there was a new intake of cadets and a new batch of commissioned pilots graduated. This made excellent sense as it ensured a steady flow of newly trained pilots entering the operational units of the RAF. After graduation, new pilots were posted to an aircraft conversion unit and onto a squadron suited to their abilities.

I arrived at the RAF College at Cranwell in the uniform of a sergeant and was to join 58 Entry. It was comprised of forty-three cadets, of which two came from Ceylon—modern-day Sri Lanka—and two from Pakistan. The plan was to spend two academic terms as a cadet to learn the basic rules of officer training, and then to relocate to the RAF College building where a further two years would be spent as a flight cadet, learning to fly and to serve as an officer in the RAF. Trusting that everything would go according to plan, I hoped to be commissioned as a pilot in April 1953. Of the forty-three cadets who joined 58 Entry, thirty-three graduated in April 1953, a failure rate of roughly one quarter, which illustrates the professional standards required. Interestingly, the cadets who were sons of retired officers of air rank failed to graduate.

The first two terms at Cranwell were split between education across the

September 1950: 58 Entry at the RAF College.

basic fundamentals, including the requirements of navigation, learning to dress and march as an RAF cadet, and exercise. We had intensive exercise every day and all first-term cadets had to learn how to box. At the end of each cadet's first term there was a boxing competition of two rounds where the new boys displayed their skills. I had never boxed before and had two rounds with a cadet of similar size, and lost the fight. Not surprisingly, some of the bouts were pretty tough.

One of my memories is going down into a coal pit. The RAF had an unusual agreement whereby the cadets went 2,000 feet underground into a coal pit while the miners came to Cranwell and were flown at 2,000 feet in an Anson. This was an interesting idea for both parties, but I have no idea how or why the concept was implemented. In retrospect, it would be interesting to know what the miners thought of the young pilot cadets that they met. I seem to recall that they were very friendly, which is exactly what you'd expect.

We were also introduced to the pleasures of flying with about two trips a

58 Entry cadets with their flying instructors.

month in an Anson, where we were taught how to read a map and keep a flying log of our trip. In April 1951 I was elevated to become a flight cadet and relocated to 'A' Squadron in the main college building. This meant I was introduced to flying the Percival Prentice, a basic training aircraft. After ten hours with an instructor I had my first ten-minute solo flight; the instructor left the aircraft I flew one circuit and landed. In my first three months I flew forty hours, of which thirteen were solo, and all during the day. I spent most of my time stalling, carrying out forced landings, and learning the basic rules of flying.

One of the cadets in my Entry had about fifteen hours with an instructor and then set off on his one circuit but decided to go around again and again and completed seven circuits before he could be persuaded to land. His name was Gamini Goonesa, one of the cadets from Ceylon and the most capable sportsman I have ever known. Unfortunately his flying failed to meet the required standards so he left the RAF College and went to play cricket for Nottinghamshire County and then Cambridge University. He later represented Ceylon on many occasions. Interestingly another friend who was also a very fine sportsman and played cricket for Kent failed to qualify as a pilot and became a navigator. I have always thought that the skills of being a capable pilot must be

Cadet Goodall flying the Prentice at the RAF College at Cranwell.

similar to being a successful sportsman, but it seems that is not the case.

After about fifty hours we commenced night flying with very similar procedures, apart from aerobatics. In 1952 the Prentice was being phased out with the introduction of the Chipmunk, which was a pleasure to fly. In May 1952, after a year flying the basic trainer, we were upgraded to flying the advanced trainer, namely the Harvard, which was a far more complex aircraft. In the Prentice you sat alongside your instructor but in the Harvard the cadet was in the front seat with the instructor behind. Another feature of this aircraft was that the engine obstructed the forward view so that you were constantly changing direction as you taxied. I had six hours' dual instruction in the Harvard and then went solo and passed the various checks.

Training was intense but not without its minor amusements. During flights the instructor would check our navigation skills by asking us to identify a particular town. On one occasion I studied my map but could not find anything that looked remotely like the town I was flying over; it turned out that the maps we were using were printed in the 1930s and my mystery town—Corby—had expanded and was not recorded on my map. It's hardly surprising that I was lost. On another occasion my instructor said, 'your engine

Cadet Goodall flying the Chipmunk.

has failed—do a dead stick landing'. I selected a large field and approached to land. By the side of a field was a haystack and, as we came in we noticed a couple making love on top of it, so we circled and waved—unfortunately the plane was not fitted with a camera. One day in October I was sent off on a solo flight and the weather deteriorated; in a trip of two hours and thirty minutes, I spent two hours and twenty minutes in cloud waiting for instructions. I have no record of the height I was flying, but at one moment, looking upwards, I caught sight of the top of a church steeple—I immediately climbed to a safe height. Eventually I was given the bearing to divert to RAF Marham, which was not too far away. When I examine my log book, I note that I went on a night cross-country flight of over two hours in the days when there was no radar to tell you where you were. I presume we were sent in good weather so that we could navigate visually.

Just before our graduation we all went off on a two-and-a-half-hour cross-

58 Entry Graduation Parade at RAF College in April 1953.

country flight to RAF Shawbury. We flew in pairs with one cadet the pilot and the other the navigator. I flew with fellow cadet John Pack and on the return flight via Doncaster I was the navigator. During the flight, one of my colleagues in a Harvard apparently made a navigational error which resulted in a shortage of fuel. They were forced to land in a field but the cadet flying the aircraft misjudged the approach, resulting in an accident in which the pilot, one of our foreign cadets, was killed. He was my Pakistani roommate and a good friend. He used to get up every morning, face east, and go through his religious procedures—he taught me a lot about Islam. This was the only fatal accident at Cranwell during my time as a cadet. I have always wondered if there was a professional enquiry into the accident and how it was assessed. Presumably the cadet navigating the aircraft, who survived the accident, was responsible for the failure to return to RAF Cranwell.

During these years, the RAF was not only training pilots but also officers

Air Chief Marshal Sir Hugh P. Lloyd, KCB, KBE, MC, DFC, LL.D inspecting the 58 Entry Graduation at the RAF College, April 1953.

who needed to do the 'right' things. There was a selection of many sports and pastimes to take part in. Activities included football, cricket, rugby, tennis, squash, boxing, swimming, and riding. I had never ridden a horse but I joined the riding club which conveniently meant that I had to be excluded from the morning drill session. We had holidays similar to a school or university and were encouraged to participate in the various activities.

In July 1951 I visited RAF Abingdon on a parachute training course. We did two drops from a tower about 800 feet tall and two from a Hastings aircraft. For the tower jump we stood on the edge one at a time, jumped out and fell for about 200 feet before the parachute opened. The hard part was landing without damaging your legs or ankles. On board the Hastings we were thrown out into the sky and had no sensation of falling until the parachute opened; then all we could hope for was a safe landing.

There were two groups of cadets at Abingdon: one from Cranwell and the other from Sandhurst. When the 'others' were learning about parachuting we went into their accommodation and swapped all the beds and their equipment. Not to be outdone, on the following day they took all of our beds and repositioned them on the main parade ground. The station commander must have gone mad at the behaviour of these 'things', as he called us, that were training to be officers.

Later in July I went down to Hamble and joined three other cadets on the yacht *Lerche*. We cruised around the south coast to Lymington and Yarmouth and had the pleasure of a Group Captain as skipper. He was the best chef I have ever met and he introduced us to many different dishes, all excellently cooked. I believe he enjoyed his role as a chef rather more than as a skipper. After this

The tower at RAF Abingdon from which we jumped during our parachute training course in 1951.

success, the next summer we decided to do the same; a party of five of us went down to Hamble for a two-week trip on the *Goldammer* to France and around the Normandy coast. Unfortunately things did not go as smoothly as the previous year. On 15 August 1952 we got caught in a storm of extraordinary power. Thankfully we were saved by a French freighter which remained with us all night. In the morning a tug arrived from Le Havre to take us back to port, where we got a boat back to England, leaving *Goldammer* at Le Havre for the insurance company to resolve. The 15–16 August 1952 was the date of the Lynmouth disaster in Devon when thirty-four people were killed and 420 made homeless. Luck was obviously on our side. The *Daily Express* reported the dreadful tragedy of Lynmouth but there was also a Reuters report:

> Crippled in crash. The RAF yacht *Goldammer* manned by five cadets and an officer was towed into Le Havre today leaking and with a broken mast. The damage was done when heavy seas threw her against a French freighter that lay alongside thinking she was in trouble.

In the 1951 Christmas holiday, a party from Cranwell went skiing at Méribel les Allues in France. For most of us it was our first skiing experience, but we all enjoyed the excellent facilities. We were enjoying a light snack in one of the many bars on the slopes when a French woman screamed—we turned round to see a Squadron Leader of our party lying on the ground with one of his legs pointing in a particularly unnatural direction. We rushed over to assist and managed to calm the woman down, informing her that leg in question was artificial—the result of the Squadron Leader's wartime operations. Fortunately we had him standing again in no time.

During our three years at Cranwell, we enjoyed our social life and naturally met young people of the opposite sex. There happened to be three teacher training colleges in close proximity and in those days they were exclusively female, though I gather that has now changed. Three of my contemporaries married young teachers and I had the pleasure of being best man to John Pack, who remained a close friend of mine after Cranwell.

I was friendly with a young lady who I recall as Betty; she invited me to her graduation ball at her college at Stoke Rochford, near Grantham. Unfortunately, the event was on a Wednesday—as cadets we were required to eat in the college on weekday evenings and our attendance was always checked. However, there was always a way round regulations. There was a hanger that was used as a garage for cadets to leave their cars; I obtained the keys, unlocked the door and returned them, leaving the door unlocked. I went to the evening meal, was checked in, and then vanished to the toilet where I remained until the dinner had commenced. I then went up to my room, changed into my dinner jacket, walked to the garage, collected my car, and drove to Stoke Rochford. After a thoroughly enjoyable graduation ball, I drove back to Cranwell, parked my car, locked the garage, and crept back to my room, satisfied with an evening well spent. In retrospect Betty and I never met again even though the Ball was a memorable event. I wonder why?

Apart from training, most cadets had other responsibilities—mine were editing the college journal and presiding over the debating society. One of the cadets who represented the college boxing team had received a blow on his ear which threatened his medical fitness to fly. Boxing suddenly became the 'do not participate' sport. An RAF Regiment Wing Commander was in charge of boxing and he phoned me and asked if we could hold a debate on boxing. Everything was agreed and the notices displayed. I received a phone call to report to the assistant commandant immediately—'You are questioning the authority of College,' he said. I explained that the officer responsible for boxing had requested the debate. I was told we could have our debate about boxing, but not about boxing in the RAF. We had a most enjoyable evening with everyone expressing their highly philosophical views, which ended with about 95 per cent opposed to boxing—a view that I still support.

As cadets we were all required to write a thesis; I found it an interesting challenge and researched the problems of war. My thesis was titled *The History of Strategic Thought* and I was awarded the Royal United Service Institution Award. It is interesting to reflect that the institution was formed by Arthur Wellesley, the 1st Duke of Wellington, in 1831—presumably he believed that future military leaders should be educated to understand the difficulties of fighting a war. The institution has now expanded its studies to include security, which would seem to be one of the greatest challenges of the twenty-first century.

When our Entry graduated on 14 April 1953 there were a number of awards handed out. The Sword of Honour was a prestigious prize awarded to the cadet assessed as the best cadet of the Entry, and there was a prize for the best pilot of the Entry. I won the Air Ministry Prize for Imperial and War Studies. The reviewing officer for the passing out of 58 Entry was Air Chief Marshal Sir Hugh P. Lloyd KCB, KBE, MC, DFC, LL.D, the late Air Officer Commanding of Bomber Command, and he offered some interesting advice:

In talking to you today, I want to place emphasis on one word. That word is 'flying'. Behind every pilot in our service there are 400 people on the ground and all of them have but one object in view—flying [...] All good airmen are enthusiasts. They tackle their flying with determination, zest and energy [...] My second point is the importance of keeping up your flying. During the next few years you will not encounter difficulties with flying because your job will be with flying units, but as you get older more ground jobs will come your way and it will become increasingly difficult to arrange your flying [...] At one time staff officers were supposed to fly in any obsolescent

Passing Out Parade held at the RAF College, Cranwell. Believed to be 57 Entry graduating in December 1952.

aircraft so that we could put our latest aircraft into squadrons [...] Airmen are needed just as much on staffs as in squadrons, and with the advent of the jet engine, this is most important. In fact orders to jet squadrons written by a staff officer who is ignorant of jet flying might just as well be written in Chinese. A piston-engined pilot today is as much out of date as an archer from Agincourt [...] My next point is that flying costs an awful lot of money. A Canberra, for example, burns 400 gallons an hour. Consequently flying must have an object and a purpose. My last point is that years ago a pilot was looked upon as a rather wild young man with dash and energy and probably little else. Today, however our flying demands not only courage but skill, accuracy and concentration of the highest order. When you go out into Service your jobs will be varied; it may be to drop a bomb, shoot a gun or take photographs, but whatever it is we must bring to it enthusiasm skill and a determination to be meticulously accurate in all we do [...] And now I must conclude. You have had the finest training in the world. The Royal Air Force wants you. Be sure throughout your career that the Service will continue to want you. It is up to you. Good luck and good fortune.

When I read that speech today it brings home the meaning and understanding of 'leadership', but when I examine the behaviour and decisions of our politicians, I understand why our country has so many major problems.

Our graduation ball on 14 April 1953 was a happy event for all the cadets of 58 Entry, and after it we were all dispatched on the next phase of our RAF careers. I only ever served with two of my Cranwell Entry—John Pack and Alan Ginn—and I was the only cadet in my Entry to be posted to Bomber Command, which is the world in which I spent my entire RAF career. When

Passing Out Parade held at RAF College, Cranwell. Believed to be 56 Entry with Princess Elizebeth as the inspecting officer.

the Vulcan came into service, John Pack re-located from Training Command to become a Vulcan co-pilot; we both commanded Vulcan squadrons at Scampton until John went off into other activities. When Alan Ginn left Cranwell, he was posted to a Meteor squadron. He was forced to bale out at a speed of about 400 knots when the aircraft he was flying developed a technical problem. At that time ejection seats did not have leg restraining straps, so his legs were blown sideways; he spent many months in hospital before returning to flying as a Valiant co-pilot. General list officers could retire at the age of thirty-eight and I believe a number of 58 Entry left at that age to pursue different careers.

When I now examine the activities of the RAF College, they seem to be totally different from my years as a cadet. If you wish to be commissioned in the RAF, it seems that you spend thirty-two weeks at Cranwell and then go to be trained in your particular speciality, whereas when I was a cadet all those

27 Squadron Vulcan XM595 taken at Tucson Air Force Base, Arizona, in March 1968.

based at Cranwell were being trained as pilots. It would seem that the talk of Air Chief Marshal Lloyd at my graduation is not relevant to the modern RAF, and I wonder how long a separate air force will exist. In April 2014, two RAF fighters based in Scotland intercepted two Russian bombers near the Scottish coast. In the politically charged run-up to the Scottish Referendum, the incident highlighted the dangers of decreasing our military strength. Maybe all politicians should be sent to the Royal United Service Institution so they have a basic understanding of defence and security.

TUPOLEV TU-95

The Tupolev Tu-95 (NATO reporting name 'Bear') has been among the main nuclear bomber types of the Soviet nuclear triad since the late 1950s. Designed as a direct successor of the Tu-4, a Boeing B-29 Superfortress non-licensed copy and the first Soviet bomber, the longer-legged new bomber was powered by four giant turboprop engines providing long range in order to reach targets in North America from airfields on Soviet territory. Based on the design of a piston-engine ultra-long-range bomber dubbed 'project 85', the new turboprop bomber sported swept wings for increased speeds. The powerplant was to include four large fuel-efficient turboprop engines, each with two four-blade counter-rotating propellers. Each of the engines rated at 15,0000 shp, and the aircraft's maximum take-off weight approached 200 tons.

The formal assignment to the Tupolev OKB to develop the new bomber ('project 95') was issued by the Soviet Council of Ministers on 11 July 1951; only seventeen months later, on 12 November 1952, the first prototype, dubbed Tu-95-1, made its first flight. It was powered by the TV-2F turboprops (eight units, arranged in four twin-engine packs), developed by the Kuznetsov OKB based on the German Jumo 022, a Second World War trophy engine. The engine was rated at 6,250 shp, and was regarded as an interim solution for use on the prototypes, while the definitive Tu-95-2 was to be powered by the TV-10 or TV-12, rated at 10,000 and 12,000 shp respectively. In order to provide the necessary power, each engine used a package of two TV-2Fs, driving two four-blade co-axial counter-rotating reversible-pitch propellers. According to the specification, its design range was to extend to 15,000 km (8,091 nm) and the cruise speed was to be between 750 and 820 kph (405 to 442 kt), with the maximum speed reaching 950 kph (512 kt). The practical ceiling was to be 14,000 m (45,920 feet). The main mission of the bomber was to conduct nuclear bombings from high altitude against the whole range of strategic targets on the territory of the possible enemy (USA and the NATO nations), otherwise unreachable for all other types of bombers fielded by the Soviet Air Force. The armament was to comprise nuclear free-fall bombs weighing up to 15,000 kg (33,060 lb). The Tu-95-1 tests, however, proved that it has much lower performance than that required by the specification due to the non-perfect airframe which was 15 per cent heavier than originally planned.

Sadly, the Tu-95-1 prototype was lost in an accident in May 1953, during its seventeenth test flight, due to engine in-flight fire. The second prototype, dubbed Tu-95-2, powered by the more powerful NK-12 turboprops, took the air on 16 February 1955. Its first public presentation took place during the Tushino Aviation Day in Moscow in the summer of the same year.

The Tu-95 completed its flight testing and was officially commissioned in Soviet Air Force service in August 1957, but the serial production began two years earlier, in 1955. It was launched in production at the GAZ-18 aircraft-building plant in Kuybishev (now Samara).

The production-standard Tu-95 weighted 172 tons and had a range of 12,100 km. An improved version, dubbed Tu-95A, was used in the nuclear role with free-fall bombs; it was equipped with temperature-controlled bomb bay and protective blinds for the windows to protect the crew from the powerful flash produced by the nuclear bomb detonation; the fuselage also received white protective paint to reflect the nuclear flash. The Tu-95A was capable of carrying the RDS-3 and RDS-4—the first Soviet nuclear bombs—and later on was made capable of carrying the RDS-6 (RDS-37) thermo-nuclear bombs. The self-defence armament comprised of six twin AM-23 23-mm cannons in three turrets—on the top and bottom fuselage and in the tail.

The Tu-95M was an improved version powered by four powerful NK-12M turboprops, each rated at 15,000 shp, while the maximum take-off weight increased to 182 tons. The range extended to 13,200 km (7,120 nm) and the maximum speed hit 920 kph (496 kt). Between 1955 and 1958, the GAZ-18 rolled out thirty-one Tu-95s and nineteen Tu-95Ms; later on, the former wer e brought to the Tu-95M standard and remained in front-line use until the mid-1980s. The survivors were finally modified for use in the training role, soldiering on until the early 1990s.

The Tu-95 was the main Soviet aircraft used for nuclear bomb testing, starting in 1958 with drops at Nova Zemlya range. These tests saw the deployment of Tu-95s taken from the front-line use for the duration of

Close view of the flight refuelling contact point.

the testing effort. After bomb drops, the aircraft returned to the base with various external damages caused by the nuclear blast, necessitating extensive repairs. Sometimes the nuclear bomb testing involved full bomber regiments for the aircrews to gain experience of operating in a real-world environment and to witness the destructive power of the nuclear explosion. A Tu-95 was used in 1960 to drop the most powerful ever thermos-nuclear air-delivered bomb with a 30-megaton yield.

In 1962, the Tu-95RTs, a reconnaissance-targeting derivative for use by the Soviet Navy, was developed; this variant was produced in fifty-three examples. The Tu-95RA was the next version built for the Soviet Air Force's long-range aviation arm. Flown for the first time in 1964, it was a dedicated reconnaissance aircraft with photo and electronic intelligence equipment, and was also the first 'Bear' version to be equipped with an air-to-air refuelling probe.

The Tu-95K, developed in the mid-1950s, was a dedicated missile-carrying version, capable of carrying a single nuclear-tipped Kh-20 air-to-surface missile suspended under the fuselage. It took to the air for the first time in January 1956 and launched its first Kh-20 missile on 6 June 1957. The Tu-95K was commissioned in Soviet Air Force service in September 1960 and stayed in production between 1958 and 1962, with forty-eight examples built. Later on the survivors were modified to the Tu-95KD version, remaining in use until the mid-1980s. Twenty-three more Tu-95KD, equipped with air-to-air refuelling probe, were built between 1962 and 1965. In the mid-1960s all Tu-95K/KD received an upgraded avionics suite in order to be capable to deploy the improved Kh-20M missile, and were re-designated as the Tu-95KM.

The T-95K-22 was a new missile-carrying version which took the air for the first time in October 1973. It was tailor-made to use the more modern Kh-22 missile, optimised for use against aircraft carriers and large coastal targets. Its testing proved to be a very protracted undertaking, with first missile firings reported in 1981 and commissioning in the Soviet Air Force service not before 1987.

The Tu-95MS is the last production version, optimised for use of the Kh-55 air-launched cruise missile, carried in a rotary launcher inside the fuselage and on wing pylons. The Tu-95MS prototype, based on the Tu-142 airframe and powerplant, took to the air for the first time in July 1978, and was kept in production between 1981 and 1992.

Another view of the flight refuelling contact point, held off the ground by the servicing crew.

4

Learning to Fly Jet Aircraft

Upon graduation from the RAF College we all continued to the next stage of our RAF careers. I was one of seven newly commissioned pilots posted to Weston Zoyland, near Bridgwater in Somerset, where we were joined by two others. We were there to learn to fly jet aircraft, specifically the Gloster Meteor, the first RAF jet fighter, which had gained the world high-speed record and was very different from flying the Harvard. The circuit speed of the Meteor was about the same as the top speed of the Harvard. As all of the former Cranwell cadets had a total of about 300 flying hours, we were anticipating a challenging few months.

Before we started flying we all had to have a High Altitude Decompression Test, which meant going into a decompression chamber where we spent one hour at 25,000 feet and one hour at 37,000 feet. Our colleague who had won the prize for the Best Pilot of the Entry suffered from decompression sickness and was lying on the floor of the chamber in unbelievable pain—it was awful to watch. Fortunately the chamber had an attached small cabin where those with a decompression problem could be brought back to the earth's normal atmospheric pressure. So the best pilot of our Cranwell Entry went off to fly piston-engine aircraft.

The Meteor was a twin-engine jet aircraft—we were not only introduced to flying a jet-powered aircraft, but also a twin-engine aircraft with the potential problem of flying it on one engine, known as asymmetric flight. There were two versions of the Meteor at Weston Zoyland: Meteor 7, the dual control aircraft with the instructor sitting behind the student, and the single-seat Meteor 4.

I had eight instructional flights in a Meteor 7 and then five solo flights in a Meteor 4. This was followed by two months of varied flying at high and low level, aerobatics, instrument flying, and even formation flying. I still recall the excitement of the low-level flying. In our low flying area there were no electric or telephone cables and wind farms had not been invented. We flew down to the south coast and then descended and flew at low level, say 200 feet at about 400 knots, back to base. It is difficult to describe the excitement and satisfaction—sadly, under today's air traffic regulations such an exercise would not be allowed. I still remember flying about 200 feet above a touring bus and have always wondered how the passengers must have reacted!

My final month's training was mainly in night flying or flying in formation at 30,000 feet, but I cannot recall why we flew in formation at such a height. In those days there was very limited radar, so if you required navigational assistance you called for a bearing. I was once sent on a night cross-country and discovered that flying at 40,000 feet is a rather lonely experience. I planned my trip and was instructed where I should call for a true bearing. Off I went and at the right time called for my bearing, only to find that I was miles off track. I checked my map and turned about 50 degrees port—left to the uninitiated—and a few minutes later called for another true bearing, but I got no response. I looked at the land below and decided I was still miles off track so I turned starboard. I waited for a few minutes and called again for a true bearing and fortunately received a reply and managed to navigate myself back to base. This flight—my last night solo in a Meteor—could easily have been the last I ever took. I had been given a reciprocal bearing 180 degrees in error, which explains why I had turned port when I called for my first true bearing. I often wonder how close I came to flying a lost Meteor somewhere into the Atlantic.

All the pilots on Course 209 at the Advanced Flying School successfully completed jet conversion training, and were sent off on their next challenging task, apart from our associate who failed the High Altitude Decompression Test. I don't know if young pilots in the twenty-first century are required to

RAF Weston Zoyland: three Meteors flying in formation with one inverted.

pass decompression tests; certainly I was never aware of any tests of a similar nature in my later years of flying.

Two of my course-mates were sent to fly the Canberra. The Meteor and Canberra are now part of RAF history and their association with the RAF highlights the changes to aircraft manufacturers and the RAF itself.

The first Meteor flew on 5 March 1943 and entered service in the RAF on 27 July. There were nineteen different models of the aircraft and almost 4,000 were built. There were sixty-three RAF squadrons and twelve Fleet Air Arm squadrons flying the Meteor. Exports are also interesting: Argentina purchased 50 new and 50 ex-RAF, Australia 104, Belgium 371, Brazil 62, Canada 2, Denmark 46, Egypt 30, and Netherlands 220.

The history of the Canberra is also fascinating. Its first flight was on 13 May 1949 and it was retired from the RAF fifty-seven years later in 2007. It had a top speed of 470 knots and achieved a world high-altitude record in 1957. Nine hundred and one Canberras were built in the UK and forty-eight in Australia. There were twenty-seven different versions which equipped thirty-five RAF squadrons. The aircraft was exported to fifteen countries, namely Australia, Argentina, Chile, Ecuador, Ethiopia, France, India, New Zealand, Pakistan, Peru, Rhodesia, South Africa, Sweden, Venezuela, and West Germany. In the United States, 403 Canberras were manufactured under licence by the Martin Aircraft Company.

I once met a Sikh doctor in India whose father had been killed flying a Canberra in the Indian Air Force; it truly was a universal aircraft and despite this sad incident, it was far safer to fly than the Meteor. In the cemetery in Weston Zoyland there are the graves of thirteen RAF personnel who died in 1952–55, of whom I believe twelve were pilots flying the Meteor. When I was learning to fly jet-powered aircraft, I had no idea of the problems that had been experienced flying the Meteor and particularly the related problems of asymmetric flight. If you were flying the Meteor on one engine and the speed dropped, increasing the engine power could cause the aircraft to rotate with tragic consequences. As pilots being trained to fly jet aircraft, we had no concept of the inherent problems of the Meteor.

5

Flying the Canberra and Joining No. 90 Squadron

On completion of my jet conversion, I was posted to No. 231 Operational Conversion Unit, based at RAF Bassingbourn just north of Royston and south-west of Cambridge. This was the base for conversion to fly the Canberra, the new aircraft entering service. At that time there were no dual-control Canberras—the B-2 version was the only Canberra in service, which meant that my first solo flight would be the first time I actually flew the aircraft. It was an interesting challenge for a pilot with my limited flying experience. The B-2 Canberra had a crew of three—a pilot and two navigators—who were all seated on Martin Baker ejection seats. The responsibility of navigation was divided between the 'plotter' and 'observer'. There was a seat alongside the pilot where a passenger could watch the performance of the pilot. The passenger would wear a parachute but leaving the aircraft in an emergency could be a problem.

Having received my jet conversion on the Meteor but not having flown the aircraft for a couple of months, my first flights were Meteor refreshers. Following four flights during daylight, I had to be checked at night. My instructor and I completed our checks and started the aircraft, but I realised then that the transmitter in my helmet was not working correctly. My instructor told me that he had a spare helmet which he rushed off to collect. We took off for my first night refresher in the Meteor 7, which was not a pressurized aircraft. At about 20,000 feet I began to feel a bit odd, so I checked my helmet and realised that my instructor had given me one without an oxygen tube—I was flying at 20,000 feet without being connected to oxygen. We rapidly descended to a level where the absence of an oxygen connection was not a serious problem.

All pilots being trained to fly the Canberra had a couple of flights on the passenger seat where the instructor demonstrated the capabilities of the aircraft from stalling to high speed flights, steep turns, radar approaches, and all handling issues. The instructor then handed over and I set off on my first flight. It must have been a challenge for the navigator as he was a passenger witnessing the first Canberra flight by the pilot—but at least he was sitting on an ejector seat. It was a wonderful aircraft to fly and I still remember my first flight where I failed to reduce the power and suddenly we were flying at very high speed.

I enjoyed an interesting and varied training schedule with an introduction to the Gee-H navigation system and dropping practice bombs. At this stage, half my flying was at night. I completed sixty hours in the Canberra and was then off to join my first squadron. I recalled the Air Chief Marshal's speech at my graduation parade at Cranwell, when he said a Canberra burns 400 gallons an hour; during my training at Bassingbourn I used about 25,000 gallons—it obviously costs a lot to train jet pilots!

After the Second World War, the United States loaned B-29s to the RAF, which we called the Washington, but it was with the introduction of jet engines that the RAF really began to change. In January 1954 I was posted to RAF Marham to join No. 90 Squadron, which was transferring from the Washington to the Canberra B-2. That month I had a trip on the last operational flight by a Washington; we flew for five hours over Belgium and

Aircrew outside the Officers' Mess at RAF Marham in 1954 prior to an air display. An advert in a local paper read: 'Don't all rush at once girls but these are your hosts for Saturday!'

Germany. The change meant a totally different Marham, with wartime aircrew leaving the service and the arrival of many younger pilots and navigators trained to fly the Canberra.

The Washington crews were to fly the aircraft back to the United States and then return to the UK for their new role. They flew to the west coast of the UK and then set off across the Atlantic, destined for Arizona. Tragically, one aircraft crashed at night at Llanarmon-yn-lai in Denbighshire with the loss of the entire crew of ten. My first job at Marham was to inspect the rooms of the three NCOs who had lost their lives and examine the entire contents. The RAF wished to ensure that the bereaved wives, parents, or girlfriends did not receive any letters or other objects that might damage the memory of those who had been killed. I made sure that the many items sent to wives or parents did not include anything which might cause a family problem. I previously had no idea of this RAF policy but it certainly was ethically correct.

As a cadet at Cranwell I had my own room, but at Marham I had to share my room with a navigator. He was a young man called Mike Burton who had been trained as a navigator and had been flying the Washington. I discovered that he was the son of a French musician and born Michel Jean-Claude de Lattre Tolis, but in 1940 his mother came to England and Mike changed his name and became an RAF navigator.

One evening, flying the last aircraft in a major exercise and coming in to land, I was informed that a Canberra had called 'Finals' but had not landed. I approached with care but saw no sign of the missing aircraft. When I got back to my room I woke Mike and told him that it looked as though a Canberra had crashed on the approach. He got dressed and went to join the fire service and the police who intended to look for the aircraft at first light. They found the aircraft near the base with the pilot still in his ejection seat. Mike was told that he could not go near the aircraft as the ejection seat presented a danger. He responded by saying that it looked as though the pilot was still alive and he would endeavour to get him out. Mike released the pilot from his live ejection seat but sadly he did not survive. This courageous action was typical of Mike—a very fine person who became a close friend. The accident was due to a runaway actuator which meant that the pilot lost control of the aircraft as the electronics directed the aircraft towards the ground. The accident was not due to a pilot error.

During the war, Bomber Command crews had difficulty in navigating to their targets as there were no navigational aids other than a system known as Gee-H. It enabled crews to log on to Gee-H transmitters and monitor their position. A bearing from two transmitters would enable the navigator to establish the aircraft's position. The system was also used for practice bombing. We spent our time dropping 25-lb or 100-lb bombs on targets located either visually or using Gee-H. These targets included Chesil Bank and Sandbanks—they wouldn't be so appropriate for practice bombing today. On one October evening we had been dropping 25-lb bombs and had half an hour to spare, so I decided I would visit my girlfriend who lived in Bath. We checked the heights and I dived down over Bath at about 400 knots, then pulled away and returned for a second visit before returning to base. I phoned my girlfriend and she slammed it down; I still have three newspaper cuttings, 'Scream in the night'. Eventually it was decided that it was a Gloster test pilot flying the Javelin.

When I joined the squadron it was interesting to work with a US Air Force Exchange Officer, Captain Lacouture. We had both been trained at a military academy and became friends. As marching procedures were obviously different, the Americans were excused from RAF parades. However, an event came round when Captain Lacouture was the most senior officer and he volunteered to lead the squadron parade. I was instructed to brief him on the marching rules of the RAF. When he was acting as the Squadron Commander he gave the instruction, '90 Squadron Quick Step March.' The concealed laughter fortunately prevented the squadron from dancing past the inspecting officer.

Captain Lacouture and his charming wife were living off base and were then allocated a married quarter. He was informed that for the past two years his quarter had won the Station Gardens Competition, established to ensure that those living in married quarters maintained their gardens and were always neat and tidy. He asked for my advice and I suggested that we visit a garden centre, if they used such names sixty years ago. We explained the problem and the most helpful expert suggested that my American associate should hire some plants for about two months to ensure an attractive garden. The garden looked superb but the 'workers' had no idea that all the plants were something rather special. When Captain Lacouture won the competition he was horrified to discover that he could be accused of cheating by hiring plants.

In the Easter and summer holidays, Chipmunks would be flown into Marham so that Air Training Corps cadets could be shown the wonders of flying. Many of the Canberra pilots spent their weekends enjoying the fun of flying. We would fly for two hours which enabled four ATC cadets to have half an hour's flying each. We had no wish to frighten young cadets so we gave them an easy and enjoyable flying experience. When one session was coming to an end we were asked to go into the Air Traffic Control Tower where we could watch the displays, however, the officer in charge had decided to dress up as an ATC cadet and fly with a friend, one Eric Brown. He would transmit so that we could listen to the 'chat' between instructor Brown and the cadet. We all spent half an hour in fits of laughter: he did everything wrong, starting by freezing the controls as if he was frightened, then playing with the throttle, the rudders, ailerons, and eventually they landed. Eric got out to give a 'mild' lecture to the cadet and was just a little surprised to see a laughing Chief Instructor. The discussion should have been recorded as it would have sold for a fortune.

In January 1955 I was one of four RAF aircrew sent to the United States Air Force in Europe (USAFE) Survival School at Bad Tolz in Germany. I still have the post card I sent to my mother where I expressed my concern at the manner in which I was being 'inspected' by the Germans while waiting in Cologne in the uniform of an RAF pilot.

We were sent on a two-week course. During the first week we were briefed on the expected behaviour of POWs. The course had been set up after the Korean War when the Americans became concerned at the number of American prisoners who had died in captivity in comparison with the British, Turkish, Australians, and New Zealanders. We were informed that roughly 2 per cent of British and Turkish prisoners had died, whereas the American losses in POW camps were around 50 per cent. We were questioned about the Second World War. Which service had a record of attempting to escape? The RAF. Which service had written books about escaping from Germany? The RAF. We had to ensure that the honour and professional standards of the RAF were upheld.

During the second week we were taken into the forests of Germany where we had to survive and attempt to escape. Each evening we were given a contact point where our 'guide' gave us some water, a couple of chocolate bars, and directions to the next contact point. After four days we were told the boundary through which we had to escape. I was the only RAF prisoner who managed to 'escape'. I was taken to the headquarters to watch the prisoners being interrogated through a one-way mirror. I watched the prisoners being interviewed by a helpful person who offered them tea and biscuits and then a shouting officer who threatened them. Military prisoners are supposed to give their number, rank, and name and nothing else, but the information passed by some of the 'prisoners' was unbelievable. It was a fascinating course but I understand that a number of US officers complained to their politicians and the course was cancelled.

At about the same time, I received a letter telling me to report to No. 3 Group Headquarters which had responsibility for RAF Marham. I arrived and was duly interviewed by an intelligence officer who informed me that I had been selected to join an intelligence team. I was to have a unique password and would be required to correspond with an intelligence officer serving at the Headquarters of No. 3 Group, Bomber Command, about once a month, and he would reply using the same code. Let us assume that my password was 'bomber command'. The letters in 'bomber' are the 2nd, 15th, 13th, 2nd, 5th, 18th, *etc.* letters in the alphabet. I was required to write a normal letter where the 2nd, 15th, 13th *etc.* letters passed the message to my recipient. It was modestly difficult to write a normal letter formulated to have the message laid out in the appropriate order. Invent your own password and see how long it takes.

Our flying was aimed at improving our skills and capability with the result that in February 1955, my crew obtained a select classification, which presented unbelievable opportunities. In March we went on our first five-day Lone Ranger flying to Idris in Libya, Fayid in Egypt, Aden which is now in Yemen, Khartoum in Sudan, back to Idris, and home to Marham. On these trips over Africa we had no navigational aids and I was flying up to eight hours a day in an aircraft without auto pilot. For example, on 11 March we flew from Khartoum to Idris in just over four hours. The aircraft was checked and refuelled before we set off on a return flight to Marham, landing that night. It demonstrates the difference between flying in the RAF in those days and civil flying—a civil pilot today would connect the auto pilot soon after take-off and credit hours in his log book.

Back at base we resumed our normal training of practice bombing. When you are flying for three-plus hours it makes sense to have a 'leak' before take-off.

PJG and a Canberra B2, ready for a trip overseas.

Lone Ranger, September 1955. PJG is fitting the starter cartridge to the Canberra. The flight was Marham–Idris–Amman–Entebbe–Nairobi–Aden–Amman–Idris–Marham. The navigator was Flying Officer Wilkinson.

On one trip I was desperate. We had a pee tube attachment to the left of the pilot; flying the aircraft with one hand, releasing the straps on my ejection seat, and accepting the rude remarks from the crew behind me took some time, but eventually I succeeded. I went to put the pee tube back and realised that I had been urinating into the metal tube and the plastic bag, which should have been attached, was nowhere to be seen. When we landed the ground crew opened the entrance door and noticed the damp floor in the aircraft. The NCO in charge put his fingers into the fluid and then into his mouth to see if he could identify the source of the leak—I must admit, that is something I have ever attempted!

Apart from exciting trips overseas, we had many routine responsibilities. When an aircraft had received a major servicing, we were required to carry out an air test to make sure it was safe to fly on overseas sorties. On one occasion I carried out the normal tests and landed the aircraft, only to be told by Air Traffic Control that I had landed in the wrong direction on the main runway. Apparently a change in wind direction had resulted in a change in the direction of landing—fortunately there were no other aircraft involved. In my report on the aircraft, I stated that it was unserviceable as it landed in the wrong direction on the runway. The engineering staff were mystified by my report but I explained that I was attempting to be humorous. Apparently it was not very funny.

In May the squadron went on a one-week detachment to Gibraltar. The runway has since been extended, but in 1955 with sea at both ends accurate landings were essential. The runway is situated very close to the Spanish border, so we had to ensure that we obeyed every flying regulation. We flew over Algeria and Morocco, which actually included practice bombing over French Morocco. We were permitted to visit La Linea in Spain provided we did not stay overnight; I suppose someone was concerned about the attractive ladies in La Linea. I can recall that we drank sherry which cost us two pence a glass. We were also entertained by the important people in Gibraltar and enjoyed meeting the mountain populace—the monkeys, or I believe technically apes as they had no tails.

In June we were away on another Lone Ranger to Idris in Libya, Khartoum, Nicosia in Cyprus, Habbaniya in Iraq, Amman in Jordan, Fayid in Egypt, Idris and home. The Habbaniya airfield was built by the British in 1934 and was a camp of great beauty with eucalyptus trees, ornamental gardens, and beautiful lawns. Control of the airfield passed to Iraq in May 1955, so I am surprised that we were able to visit it when we did. When we visited Amman we were permitted to fly a sortie at low level over the desert sands and hills, a landscape which has been fixed in my memory ever since.

As the summer months are the time for air displays, we were practising our formation flying in preparation for Farnborough, the Battle of Britain,

A Canberra B2 with its crew's luggage.

and visiting dignitaries such as the Sultan of Muscat. Then in September came another tour of the Middle East; Idris in Libya, Amman in Jordan, Aden in Yemen, and Nairobi in Kenya. The weather at Nairobi was awful with solid cloud up to 40,000 feet; there were also no landing aids in Nairobi, so we were diverted to Entebbe in Uganda. When the weather cleared we flew to Nairobi, then Aden in Yemen, Abu Sueir in Egypt, Idris in Libya, and home to Marham. We flew two trips a day, so over six hours flying, with refuelling, briefings, and weather checks, which meant a very long day. The breadth of our destinations around the world illustrate the military importance of Great Britain back in the 1950s.

When I joined No. 90 Squadron, my squadron commander was Squadron Leader R. G. Wilson, known to everyone as Bob. He left the squadron to be appointed the 'A' Flight Commander of No. 138 Squadron, which was to be the first Valiant squadron in the RAF. The squadron was formed in February 1959 at RAF Gaydon, an airfield just south of Warwick. Gaydon was to become the Valiant Operational Conversion Unit where all Valiant crews

An RAF crew boarding a Valiant.

would be trained. In May 1955, the squadron moved to RAF Wittering, which was the first V-Force base. Wittering is just south of Stamford in Lincolnshire.

With the introduction of four-engine jet aircraft into service, all the pilots were experienced. The co-pilots would spend six months in the right-hand seat and then be appointed captains, thus it was ensured that there would be minimal problems in a completely new generation of aircraft. In the summer of 1955, Squadron Leader Wilson led the first Valiant trip to the Far East with two Valiants flying to Iraq, Pakistan, Ceylon, Singapore, Australia, and New Zealand. As the Valiants had only been in service for about four months, this was an exciting venture.

Rumour had it that there was a problem with one of the co-pilots in No. 138 Squadron. In October, I was posted to Gaydon on No. 1 Second Pilots' Course with the intention of joining Squadron Leader Wilson as his co-pilot.

VICKERS VALIANT

The Vickers Valiant was the first of the three V-bombers to become operational, the first to drop a nuclear bomb, the first to see action in a conventional bombing role, and the first to be decommissioned from service with the RAF.

In the aftermath of the Second World War, the perceived threat of Soviet aggression in Europe was the driving force behind British military

A Valiant crew running to their aircraft.

planning. In 1947, the Ministry of Supply issued Specification B.35/46, calling for a bomber capable of flying close to the speed of sound, reaching an altitude of 50,000 feet, and carrying a nuclear bomb. It demanded an extraordinary leap forward in design and technology from the piston-engined bombers of the Second World War. By commissioning more than one aircraft in response to a single Operational Requirement, the Air Ministry wanted to guarantee against failure by spreading the odds, despite the extra cost. Avro and Handley Page matched the Specification with advanced designs, but Vickers fell short. However, Vickers chief designer George Edwards was able to convince the Air Ministry to accept the Vickers design as a stopgap before production aircraft for the more complex Avro and Handley Page designs became available.

The first prototype (WB210) for jet bomber Vickers Type 660 took to the air in May 1951. Type 660, renamed 'Valiant' a month later, was a conventional, 'unfunny' design, as described by Edwards, with a shoulder-mounted wing and four Rolls-Royce Avon RA.3 turbojet engines buried in the wing roots. It met the original Specification in its 54,000-foot service ceiling and its ability to carry a 10,000-lb nuclear bomb, but it was short on speed, with a maximum of 567 mph.

On 12 January 1952, WB210 was lost in a crash caused by an in-flight fire. All but one of the five-man crew escaped—the co-pilot collided with the tail after ejecting and received fatal injuries. Despite this tragedy, complete disaster was averted as the second Valiant prototype was close to completion. With a modified fuel system, upgraded Avon RA.7 engines, and enlarged engine intakes, WB215 took to the air on 11 April 1952.

The first production Vickers Valiant B.1 aircraft flew on 21 December 1953 and was delivered to the RAF on 8 February 1955. The Valiant B.2 prototype was developed as a low-flying 'Pathfinder' to be used as a target marker. It had a lengthened fuselage and a strengthened airframe to cope with the increased strain of low-level flying, and was fitted with higher performance Rolls-Royce Conway engines. The Air Ministry ordered seventeen B.2s, but the order was cancelled in 1955 when advances in radar rendered Pathfinder tactics obsolete. However, the B.2 prototype, completed in September 1953, continued to be used for test flights and air displays until 1958.

On 1 January 1955, No. 138 Squadron was equipped with the Vickers Valiant; six months later the squadron moved from RAF Gaydon to RAF Wittering, where the RAF was stockpiling its nuclear weapons. In 1956,

five more Valiant squadrons were formed, and in October of that year, Valiant B.1 WZ366 dropped a down-rated Blue Danube nuclear bomb over Maralinga, South Australia. Britain's first nuclear test was a success: V-bomber force was now operational.

October 1956 also saw the Valiant in action for the first and only time, although in a conventional role rather than a nuclear attack. President Nasser's occupation of the Suez Canal in July led to an Anglo-French operation to retake the canal in cooperation with Israeli forces. The Air Ministry saw it as a good opportunity to test their new strategic bomber and Valiants of Nos 138, 148, 207, and 214 Squadrons were deployed to an airfield in Luqa, Malta. During Operation Musketeer in October and November 1956, RAF Valiants dropped 842 tons of bombs on Egyptian military targets, coming up against no serious resistance and incurring no casualties. The results, however, were disappointing—only three of the seven airfields targeted were damaged severely.

In 1957, Valiant production ceased while the other V-bombers—the Avro Vulcan and the Handley Page Victor—became operational. The shooting down of Gary Powers' U-2 spy plane over Russia in May 1960 changed the way the Air Ministry planned to attack Soviet Russia, and the Valiant was belatedly converted to a low-level strategic bomber. However, this was a role for which the abortive Valiant B.2 had been designed, not the B.1. While the more advanced Vulcan and Victor adapted with ease, the Valiant struggled to cope with the turbulent conditions at low altitude. In August 1964, following an incident in which a wing of a Valiant was found to be sagging mid-flight, an emergency inspection was called for all Valiants in service. Severe stress fractures in the wing spars were discovered on the majority of aircraft, and the entire RAF Valiant fleet, numbering fifty aircraft at the time, was grounded in December 1964.

With the other two V-bombers performing well, it was decided that the cost of repairing or replacing the wing spars on the Valiant fleet was too great. It was a sudden and premature end for an aircraft that had once been the spearhead of the British nuclear deterrent. Most of the aircraft were scrapped at their bases, some were used as fire training airframes, and only one, XD818, was kept for preservation. It can now be seen with examples of the other two V-bombers at the RAF Museum, Cosford.

Opposite above: An airborne Valiant from below.

Opposite below: Valiant with ground crew carrying the flight refuelling cable.

6

No. 138 Squadron—Valiant Co-Pilot

I spent two months at RAF Gaydon learning all about the Valiant, which included two familiarisation flights, and then joined No. 138 Squadron at RAF Wittering in November 1955. The Valiant had only been in service for a matter of months, so we spent all our flying on trials, testing the new radar and other equipment which would be in service for some thirty years. In particular the new navigation system known as Navigation and Bombing System (NBS), which allowed the aircraft to navigate and bomb targets without any connection to other radars. In April 1956 we were distracted from our usual training by formation flying to impress Bulganin and Khrushchev, who were visiting the UK.

Over the next three months we were involved in trials testing the new equipment coming into service. If the Valiants were to be used in a conventional war, the crews had to be trained to drop bombs. As the new radar bombing system was still being developed and was not yet fitted to most aircraft, the Valiants had to be provided with a bomb aiming capability, thus they were immediately equipped with a visual bombsight similar to that used in the Second World War. High altitude visual bombing became the order of the day, and we were dropping practice bombs on every available bombing range in the UK.

In August 1956, the routine of my crew was suddenly changed when my skipper, Squadron Leader Bob Wilson, was tasked to establish that Valiants could operate from RAF Luqa in Malta. We flew out to Malta and carried out a full-load night take-off. This operation highlighted two serious problems: Luqa was the only airfield with a suitable runway from which the Valiants could operate, and none of the 1,000-lb bombs in Malta were compatible with the Valiant. Fortunately the Canberra used a similar bomb, so the Canberra crews unexpectedly found themselves ferrying bombs out to Malta. The Canberra carried six 1,000-lb bombs, whereas the Valiant had the capability of carrying twenty-one. It was an expensive way of sending 1,000-lb bombs to Malta, but the operation was completed in a matter of days.

In October 1956 there were only four Valiant Bomber squadrons, and some

The Valiant at take off.

of them were still being equipped with new aircraft, which meant that the total force available was just twenty-four aircraft. There was frenzied activity on No. 138 Squadron as we made up a third of the total force. On 19 October we flew out to Malta.

Three months earlier, in July 1956, the world had changed. President Nasser nationalized the Suez Canal. In the recent past I have heard our historical experts talking about the Suez Campaign and the discussions between the Egyptians, French, Israelis, and the British, which differs from my recollections. The day after our arrival we were all briefed at Air Operations and I recall my surprise at seeing a large map of Israel on one wall and a map of Egypt on the other, which made us all wonder who the enemy was to be.

With only a few of the Valiants having been fitted with the new radar equipment it was decided to use Second World War techniques on the other aircraft. A Valiant fitted with the NBS radar would lead each attack and drop a red proximity marker on the selected target. Canberras operating from

RAF crew boarding a camouflaged Valiant.

Cyprus would fly at low level using the light from the proximity marker to identify the actual target and then drop a green target marker to be used as the aiming point for the bomber force. The first Valiant in each attack would drop the proximity marker and then orbit at high level to lead the bomber force to drop bombs visually on the green marker. This was not the most sophisticated or accurate means of dropping bombs from 40,000 feet and above.

There were two other aspects that surprised me. We were all issued with revolvers as a means of protection if we were shot down. We were also given a British Government Promissory Note which offered to pay a vast sum to

A Valiant captain signing paperwork prior to take off.

anyone rescuing the holder, aptly named 'gooly chit'! Unfortunately I cannot remember the financial offer, but I know they were assiduously collected after each sortie. I suppose the Air Staff were worried that if we knew we were only worth £100, we might go on strike!

On 29 October 1956 Israel invaded Egypt, and on the 30th Britain and France threatened to invade unless President Nasser withdrew from the Canal Zone. On 31 October, we were sent to bomb Egypt.

My squadron commander, Wing Commander Rupert Oakley, a highly decorated Second World War pilot, was leading the first attack planned on

Valiant flying over the sea.

Cairo West. After the force had taken off, it was discovered that the Americans had a number of Constellation aircraft at Cairo which were evacuating American citizens from Egypt. Unfortunately, nobody had planned any recall procedures, so you can imagine the panic. It so happened that the station commander of our base in the UK was part of the Operational Planning Team in Cyprus, so he called Rupert Oakley on the radio, 'Rupert, it's John here, you've got to turn back.' Fortunately the two officers recognised each other's voices, so a political disaster was avoided. The aircraft returned to Luqa and were instructed not to jettison their bombs.

Our aircraft was fitted with the new Navigation and Bombing System (NBS) so my captain was leading an attack on the Egyptian Air Force base of Abu Sueir from an altitude of 42,000 feet. As we approached Egypt all looked peaceful. The lights in the towns and cities were glimmering below. Our eyes were searching the skies for any sign of enemy aircraft. The radar operator identified the target and the call 'Target Indicator away' was made. We turned back and prepared to make our second attack with live bombs. The sky was lit up by our red proximity marker. Shortly afterwards the Canberra pilot came on the radio and said simply, 'Identified the target'. We waited for what seemed like hours but it must have been only minutes, then the sky was

Valiant crew of Squadron Leader Wilson that in October and November 1956 attacked Egypt in the Suez War. PJG (second from left) was the co-pilot. The photograph includes the Crew Chief who flew out to Malta but was not part of the crew that bombed Egypt.

lit up again but this time by the green marker, followed by instructions from the Canberra pilot, 'Bomber Force bomb on the green marker'. By this time we were running in for our second attack: 'Right, steady, right, steady, steady, bomb doors open, steady, bombs away.' All our bombs were dropped and we turned back towards Malta, followed in turn by the other aircraft on the raid. All appeared to have worked according to plan and the entire force returned to Luqa some five and a half hours after take-off.

It is interesting to reflect that in September 1955 I flew a Canberra into Abu Sueir on a training flight and in October 1956 I was bombing the same airfield—how the world changes. Should we trust our politicians? The following day, we all anticipated great publicity and applause for the new high-level air aces, only to learn of the discord and argument at home. Certainly the news had a deflationary effect on the whole force with the realisation that our operations were the cause of serious disharmony.

Nevertheless, we had a task to complete. Attacks continued for the next five days on a variety of targets, specifically seven airfields, two military barracks, a naval repair depot, and a railway marshalling yard. We bombed Huckstep Barracks on 2 November and were not aware of any defensive actions, but apparently AA fire was observed at some of the targets.

Following the six days of operations, it was evident the politicians rather than the military were fighting, so we made a quiet return to the UK on 7 November, less than three weeks after we had left home. Not surprisingly, I suppose, we were met by the press. John Cochrane, a Scottish friend and colleague, was asked how he passed his time in Malta and assured the reporter that Egyptian calisthenics was his pastime and duly earned national publicity. The RAF smiled, as in our parlance, Egyptian PT was sleeping. My crew was met by Pathé news and my mother sat through three films to see the news and I am quite certain that the whole cinema would have known that it was her son!

The report on Operation Musketeer—the Suez War—details the RAF participation. There were twenty-four Valiants operating out of Luqa, a further twenty-nine Canberras operating out of Luqa and Halfar in Malta, and fifty-nine Canberras operating from Nicosia in Cyprus. In six days of operations, a total of 259 sorties were flown and 942 tons of bombs were dropped.

I have read many articles by journalists on the Suez conflict and most are highly critical of the accuracy of the bombing by the Valiant crews. When you consider that we were bombing visually from over 40,000 feet on green markers, it is not the least surprising that it was not the most accurate bombing in history. Rather different from the accuracy of the Tornado attacks on Libya.

One of the Canberra pilots operating out of Nicosia collapsed his undercarriage to avoid operations in Egypt, but the incident received no publicity. I believe he qualified as a civil pilot. A few years ago I had an article published about the Suez War and I phoned the widow of my skipper to inform her of it. She said a copy had been sent to her and that it was the first time she had been given any idea of what her husband had been doing. When we flew out to Malta she was told to go and stay with her parents and that was all.

In some thirty-five years of operational service, the V-bombers actively participated in just two military operations—the Valiant at Suez and the Vulcan in the Falklands War.

Following the Suez operations, we continued our proving flights, testing the new equipment coming into service. We also had permanent detachments in Malta. One of our senior captains was operating from Malta when he saw a United States aircraft carrier so he thought he would have a bit of fun. He descended to low level, put his undercarriage down and made an approach to land on the US aircraft carrier. You can imagine the lights, rockets, *etc.* fired from the carrier. Apparently the Americans did not appreciate his sense of humour—nor did the senior RAF officers.

The number of young co-pilots was increasing so the Air Officer Commanding our Bomber Group, No. 3 Group, interviewed about fifteen young pilots to assess who was suitable for a captaincy. At the end of the interviews, we were told that we would all become captains over the next three years. I returned to my base and was interviewed by my squadron commander. I said that we were all considered suitable to become captains but as I was very happy on No. 138 Squadron, I had requested to transfer to the Victor. He responded by saying that was not a good idea as the Victor was way behind schedule. 'Anyway, that is not relevant as you are posted. You go on the Valiant captains' course on Sunday.'

MIKOYAN & GUVERICH MIG-21

The MiG-21 (NATO reporting name Fishbed) firmly holds the title of the world's most widely built and used jet fighter, with more than 10,000 units rolling off the lines of three plants in the former Soviet Union. The type was also built under license in India and Czechslovakia, and without license in China until the late 2000s. Designed as a Mach-2 light tactical fighter, its original prototype, the Ye-6/1, was first flown in 1958. The first production variant of the type, designated the MiG-21F, appeared in 1960, and its improved sub-variant, the MiG-21F-13 (type 74, NATO reporting name Fishbed-C), was made available for export by 1961. It was a simplified daytime short-range, clear-weather interceptor and tactical fighter.

The MiG-21's airframe design was very simple and remarkably low-drag. It was suitably combined with a lightweight and powerful afterburning turbojet, much better and more reliable than the two engines powering its MiG-19 predecessor, coupled with an all-new tailed delta-wing layout with a relatively high wing loading and a small cross-section fuselage. The successful design, featuring low structural weight and low wave drag, offered levels of performance that were very impressive for the second half of the 1950s. This was the chief reason for the MiG-21's success, underpinned by the aircraft's simplicity, reliability, and affordability.

The MiG-21F-13 was designed from the outset to intercept transonic/supersonic bombers and fighter-bombers at altitudes up to 20,000 m (65,600 feet). Its practical ceiling was 20,100 m (65,920 feet) while maintaining Mach 1.1, and the maximum level speed in afterburner was Mach 2, equal to 2,100 kph (1,133 kt) at 15,000 m (49,200 feet).

Interceptions were limited to rear-hemisphere attacks only, using the rudimentary SRD-5M Kvant radar rangefinder with a range of 0.5–7 km (0.27–3.8 nm). The Kvant provided missile launch and gun-firing distances; the associated ASP-5ND gun-sight was used to assist accurate aiming during gun- and rocket-firing runs on both air and ground targets. In real-world conditions, MiG-21F-13 intercepts were critically dependent on guidance from a ground control station—manned by a dedicated Ground Control Intercept (GCI) officer using voice commands to transfer speed, altitude, and heading data commands—until the target was visually acquired.

Its principal armament of two R-3S heat-seeking air-to-air missiles was carried on two APU-28 rail launchers, later replaced by the APU-13, attached to BD3-58-21 adaptor beams, one under each wing. The MiG-21F-13 also retained one internal NR-30 30-mm cannon on the starboard side, with only thirty rounds. The alternative ordnance in the fighter-interceptor role consisted of two UB-16-57UM rocket packs, each loaded with sixteen S-5M 57-mm rockets, instead of the R-3S missiles. These rockets were judged as an effective weapon, particularly when fired from close range against large bombers and transport aircraft, but they were ill-suited for use against manoeuvring fighters.

The R-3S (K-13) air-to-air missile was a reverse-engineered copy of the American AIM-9B Sidewinder heat-seeking AAM, with an effective range at low altitude of 0.5–2 km (0.3–1.1 nm), which at high altitude extended to 9 km (4.9 nm).

Soviet MiG-21F fighter.

Soviet MiG-21F fighter.

The MiG-21PF was the first production-standard all-weather interceptor derivative of the 'Fishbed' family, equipped with the RP-21 Sapfir-21 air-intercept radar and sporting a series of fuselage and powerplant improvements. It was originally designed as an integral component of the MiG-21P-13 air-intercept system; the radar-equipped interceptor initially received the new in-service designation MiG-21P and its production was launched in March 1960. However, it was very soon superseded by the improved MiG-21PF version. The new version introduced a vastly modified fuselage with a longer nose and a much larger intake centre body, accommodating the large radar antenna, while at the same time retaining the airflow rates required for the normal engine operation. The RP-21M radar used a single parabolic conical-scan antenna housed in the nose centre body. It featured a 15-km (8.1-nm) detection range against a fighter-size target and the tracking range was 10 km (5.4 nm), while against bombers these ranges increased up to 20 km (10.8 nm) and 15 km (8.1 nm) respectively.

The modified MiG-21PF, featuring the SPS system, underwent its state testing with the NII VVS in the first half of 1962. The blown flaps bestowed a notable improvement in landing performance: in combination with the more effective cruciform brake parachute, this novelty enabled the landing roll to be shortened to 480 m (1,574 feet), while the landing speed decreased to 249 kph (134 kt). A significant reduction in the take-off run was achieved by the means of using two SPRD-99 assisted take-off solid-fuel boosters, each developing 24.52 kN (5,500 lb st or 1,323 kgf) of thrust for 10–17 seconds.

The RS-2US (K-5) used by the MiG-21PF/PFS/PFM was a 1950s-vintage guided weapon designed originally for use with the RP-5 air-intercept radar of the MiG-19PM, and was effective only against non-manoeuvring targets. Originally built for use against bombers, its warhead weighed 13 kg (5.9 nm). The missile proved very sensitive to the radar beam shape of the launch platform and its movements, and was also prone to jamming. The effective range at low altitude was 2.5–5 km (1.3–2.7 nm), while at high altitude it extended to 6.5 km (3.5 nm).

The MiG-21PF/PFS/PFM's time to intercept a target flying at 16,000 m (52,500 feet) was eight minutes from the initial take-off run. A manoeuvring limitation of 3.5 G was imposed during the early years of MiG-21PF/PFM operations due to radar operability and reliability concerns in regard to the complex vacuum tube technology, but by the early 1970s this restriction had been lifted and the interceptor was cleared for manoeuvring with up to 8.5 G, depending on the fuel state and external stores. Owing to their weak armament of only two short-range AAMs, both the MiG-21PF and PFM variants were nicknamed the 'Peaceful Doves' in the Soviet Union and Warsaw Pact.

The MiG-21PF/PFS/PFM was in production at the GAZ-21 at Gorky for the Soviet Air Force between 1961 and 1968.

7

No. 90 Squadron—Valiant Captain

In March 1957 I found myself back at RAF Gaydon as one of two young pilots to be trained as Valiant captains. The other was my Scottish friend, John Cochrane. As I had been flying as a co-pilot for eighteen months, it was back to flying the Canberra as a captain and then sessions in the Valiant simulator before flying the Valiant. The simulator was another new piece of equipment which enabled the instructor to put the pilot through all the emergency drills. My new crew comprised a co-pilot of my age, two navigators, one with wartime flying experience, and a non-commissioned officer as signaller. If he had been commissioned he would have been an air electronics officer, but as an NCO he was a signaller. The training was mostly uneventful, apart from one occasion when my co-pilot was doing a radar approach and I was monitoring his flying. Suddenly, about 200 feet above I saw a Canberra approaching to land. We turned starboard over the airfield buildings at about 200 feet and at full power. Air Traffic asked me what I was doing and my response was, 'Look out of the window'. The Canberra pilot had arrived at Gaydon and his radio had failed, so he flew at 1,000 feet down the runway and waggled his wings to indicate that he had lost his radio contact, and then did a visual circuit to land. This was the accepted procedure of the day. As we were doing a radar approach, the Canberra pilot had no idea there was a Valiant anywhere near the airfield. There was no air traffic controller upstairs in the visual control room, so Air Traffic were unaware that a Canberra was in the circuit. Luckily I saw the Canberra or I guess it would have been a very short tour as a captain.

In June the two young aircraft captains were posted to No. 90 Squadron, based at Honington near Bury St Edmunds in Suffolk. John Cochrane and I were to remain friends throughout our lives, although our future paths would lead in very different directions. In July I joined No. 90 Squadron detachment at RAF Luqa in Malta. It was a flight of three hours and thirty-five minutes, but as the junior pilot, unfortunately I was chosen to return to base in a Beverley transport aircraft, which took nine hours and ten minutes. But while operating in Malta we carried out the usual visual and NBS practice bombing, but I have to admit that I cannot remember the targets.

In November, the wife of my navigator plotter tragically committed suicide, which meant that I was in need of a replacement navigator. My crew of Russ Rumbol, navigator radar, Ken Hunt, navigator plotter, and Gus Allen, signaller, flew together for four years and remained friends, which was not always the case by any means. In December it was back to Luqa; interestingly, we again flew over Egypt without restrictions.

Before we returned to the UK, I went to check the aircraft and found our crew chief, Chief Technician 'F' Goddard, seriously upset, but he assured me that everything was in order. About a month later I was flying in the same aircraft and the crew chief reminded me that I had shown concern in Malta. 'I was checking my aircraft,' he said, 'and I found watches hidden in there. People do not hide watches in my f****** aircraft, so I moved all the watches so that they could not be found, flew back to the UK and waited.' He later identified all the airmen who had hidden watches in his aircraft and told them that they would be court martialled if they ever repeated such actions.

This was not a completely isolated incident. A year or so later, when Valiants were making constant trips to the Middle East, a customs officer was concerned by the contents of a Diplomatic Bag—the means by which secret documents were transported—found in one of the aircraft. The bag was opened and it contained a camera which the officer responsible for the Diplomatic Bag was attempting to conceal. He was court martialled. The chairman of the court was Group Captain Johnny Johnson, the CO of RAF Cottesmore, and the lawyer defending the officer was a friend of mine called Geoffrey Beccle. Interestingly, both of these men were to honour me in very different ways.

In March 1958 the squadron was tasked to fly two Valiants to the Far East for displays in Southern Asia, specifically at Saigon in Vietnam. My squadron commander and flight commander flew the Valiants to Singapore, and my crew went out in a Comet via Egypt, Pakistan, Ceylon, and into Changi Airport in Singapore. It so happened that the detachment coincided with the twenty-first anniversary of the Royal New Zealand Air Force, so Wing Commander Len Trent VC DFC, a New Zealander, flew out to Singapore and took one of the Valiants to New Zealand, which meant that my crew would spend three weeks in Singapore with no aircraft.

My first trip was flying around Malaya and I recall doing an approach at Kuala Lumpur. All the traffic in the city seemed to have stopped and was watching the aircraft in the sky—which nobody would have ever seen before. On another trip I flew an Air Marshal serving in the Far East and we were the first jet aircraft to land at Butterworth. They were still building the airfield, and the work force had to be ordered to clear from the runway to allow us to land. We taxied back down the runway and then took off.

When a Valiant was flying, there was always a captain in the tower at

90 Squadron detachment to the Far East in March 1958. Three crews were led by Wing Commander Hazlewood, Squadron Leader Spencer, and Flight Lieutenant Goodall.

Changi airfield. One evening I was the duty captain and heard the message: 'A black Constellation will shortly land to be refuelled. Its landing and take-off is not to be recorded.' A black aircraft with no markings was refuelled and took off immediately. A few days later I was again in the tower and I heard the message: 'A black Constellation will shortly land to be refuelled. Its landing and take-off is not to be recorded.' Air Traffic instructed the Shell Office to refuel the aircraft, and I recall the response: 'Until some **** pays for the fuel we put into some non-existent aircraft, you can **** off!' The RAF agreed to pay for the fuel and I have always wondered where the aircraft was going, but I guess somewhere in Indonesia.

Life in Singapore in 1958 was totally different from Singapore today. We were advised to go to Boogie Street to have an evening meal. The matron of

90 Squadron detachment in Malaya in 1958.

the RAF hospital and the Roman Catholic priest were eating together, so we presumed we must be in the right location. The meal was superb and then at midnight the floor show began, with the most beautiful array of young girls that I have ever seen. There was only one problem, the girls were in fact boys, or so I was told!

In those days political life in Singapore and Malaya was uncertain; communists were attempting to invade Malaya. A contemporary, Paul Gray, who was in the same Entry as me at RAF Cranwell was on a helicopter squadron operating in Malaya. It operated from Fort Tapong and the crews flew up into the Malayan jungle to supply food and arms to the troops fighting the communists in the jungle. I had the unique experience of flying with Paul and landing in a tiny 'hole' in the jungle. The surrounding trees were hundreds of feet high and we just dropped into 'the hole'. I have never flown a helicopter

and have no idea how they operated successfully in the Malayan jungle.

There were some Hastings aircraft based in Changi, presumably to allow the distribution of anything or anybody that was required. I had the pleasure of being the 2nd pilot in a Hastings and flying up to Hong Kong, which was another interesting experience with the relatively short runway in 1958. It took fifteen hours of flying—only slightly less than flying home in the Valiant.

I became friendly with a nurse working in the hospital and one Sunday we drove into Malaya and up the east coast to Mersing, where there was a beautiful beach and ideal for swimming. In the early evening we decided to return and arrived at the local village where the road was closed with a barricade so that nothing could be driven through—presumably a protection from any visiting communists. I parked outside and tooted my horn, but there was no response. I locked the young lady in the car and climbed over the barricade and fortunately found someone who spoke English. I explained my

Above: Valiant crew in Malaya: Brian Warwick, PJG, Ken Hunt, Gus Allen, and Russ Rumbol.

Opposite above & below: Fort Tapong, Malaya.

problem and the barricade was removed for us to drive in, and another for us to drive out on the other side of the village. We were relieved to arrive back at RAF Changi soon afterwards.

We also enjoyed touring around Singapore, visiting sights such as the Tiger Balm Gardens, which had statues, artistic displays of monsters and dioramas apparently depicting scenes from Chinese folklore. Another service I had never seen was cycleshaws, where you are driven around in a cabin on the back of a cycle.

Our Valiant returned from New Zealand and we flew home via Katunayake in Ceylon, Karachi, Bahrein, El Adem, and home. When we arrived in Ceylon we were parked well away from the civil aircraft but an Australian Quantas crew saw an aircraft they had never seen. The captain with his gold braid and the other crew members all came over and asked if they could meet the captain. I came out of the aircraft and was told, 'No, we wish to see the captain'. I was

Opposite above: Paul Gray taking off at Tapong.

Opposite below: Officers' Club, RAF Changi.

Above: PJG with the nurse at Mersing.

a Flight Lieutenant aged twenty-seven with just two stripes on my shoulder, so I suppose they expected someone in their forties with a few more stripes!

On our return to the UK we resumed our training flights, but a new competition had been introduced, namely the RAF Bombing Competition. All the V-bomber squadrons competed for the Laurence Minot Trophy where the bombing accuracy of the crews was radar assessed. During May 1958 my crew flew in three rounds of the Bombing Competition, and by the end of the month it was back to Luqa in Malta. We spent two weeks in the Mediterranean, which included visual bombing in Libya and landing at El Adem. Back at base in the UK, we were given a new task: my crew and I had been selected to fly in the three V-bomber formation at the Society of British Aircraft Constructors Show at Farnborough in September. A Vulcan would lead the formation with a Valiant on the left and a Victor on the right. As I was flying in the formation led by the Vulcan, I flew from the right-hand (co-pilot's) seat to ensure the formation retained its appropriate stance. We

Aerial view of Valiant WD873.

Airborne photo of Valiant XD861.

formed over the English Channel and flew down to Weymouth where we turned right and flew up to Farnborough. When there is a national exhibition, such as the Farnborough Air Display, a legal documentation is sent to all those concerned, which was known as the NOTAM, Notification of Air Movement. This should mean that all other aircraft are nowhere near the display. On one of the flights I suddenly heard an explosion of rage from my navigator. As I was flying in the right-hand seat and concentrating on watching the Vulcan to ensure the safety of the formation, I had not seen a civil aircraft near by—the pilot had apparently not bothered to read the NOTAMs. The Victor captain saw the aircraft and shouted at me to pull up but failed to press the transmit button. There was later a formal enquiry and the female pilot flying the Rapide nearly lost her licence. Shortly after the SBAC show, there were the Battle of Britain shows and our formation flew to fifteen airfields. I still have a personal letter from Group Captain Johnny Johnson CB, CBE, DSO and two bars, DFC and bar, congratulating us on the excellence of our display.

A Victor crew preparing to enter their aircraft.

Receiving a congratulatory letter from one of the most famous Second World War fighter pilots was a great honour.

When we were posted to No. 90 Squadron, we were part of the UK's nuclear deterrent. At that time all the V-bombers were painted white as we were ready for a high-level penetration of the Russian air space. All the crews were required to do a monthly evaluation of their operational sorties. There were two plans: the NATO plan and the UK plan, in the unlikely event that the UK might enter a nuclear war alone.

At least once a year, crews were brought to Readiness in an Exercise Mayflight, where all serviceable aircraft were fitted with practice nuclear weapons and aircraft were dispersed to the airfields with the Operational Readiness Platforms (ORPs). It was planned that there would be nine V-bomber bases, five dispersal airfields for four aircraft, and twenty-two dispersal airfields for two aircraft, making a total thirty-six airfields with OPRs in the UK, from St Mawgan in Cornwall to Machrihanish, Argyll, in the north of Scotland. When these facts are reviewed in the twenty-first century, it emphasizes the agreement between the politicians and the military and the positive actions which were taken, which is certainly not a feature of this century. The airfields were all equipped with five-berth caravans where the V-Force crews slept close to the aircraft, which enabled the aircraft to be airborne in minutes. I have attempted to get a photograph of one of the caravans in which I slept on many occasions, but I guess they have all been destroyed.

No. 94 Maintenance Unit was based at Barnham near Honington and was responsible for constructing the RAF's nuclear weapons. A qualified young solicitor, Geoffrey Beccle, doing his national service, was posted to Barnham but lived in the Officers' Mess at Honington—our friendship changed my life. As he lived in London he persuaded me to join him to meet some interesting young ladies. It so happened that five young air hostesses shared a flat in St Peters Road in Twickenham. I became engaged to a young Scottish lady and we were married in October 1959. I asked the Air Marshal commanding our operational group if we could borrow his aircraft for the weekend. My friend, John Cochrane, was checked to fly the aircraft and on the Friday flew up to Renfrew to return on the Monday, thus many from the squadron had an enjoyable weekend in Scotland, entertained by my wife's friends. I still have a copy of the *Scottish Sunday Express* which has a photograph of us both just after our marriage. The report, entitled 'Soccer chief's daughter weds an airman' (my father-in-law was ....) reads:

Opposite above: A Victor captain talking to the crew chief.

Opposite below: A white Victor with Blue Steel.

[Her] groom was Flight Lieutenant Philip Goodall, eight of whose brother officers from RAF Honington formed a guard of honour. But they nearly didn't make it as the plane in which they were flying to Scotland yesterday developed engine trouble. An 'emergency' was signalled to Abbotsinch Airfield, but the aircraft managed to land safely.

Actually I think it was the pilot who managed to land the aircraft safely—I seem to remember that John Cochrane was very competent at the controls.

I am frequently asked what life was like living in an environment when at any moment one could be ordered on a sortie to drop a nuclear weapon on Russia. We all regarded our role as a deterrent and hoped that we would never have to carry out the threat. Despite this potential responsibility hanging over us, life at Honington in Suffolk was extremely pleasant. Married officers and airmen mainly lived in married quarters on the base, and those who had not made that momentous decision lived in the messes on the base. The sports facilities on base were excellent and we had the opportunity to participate in many activities. Historically, the RAF had built squash courts in close proximity to the Officers' Mess, so we could participate in strenuous activity to keep fit, irrespective of the weather and time of day. I had the pleasure of running the squash team and we had the satisfaction of winning the Bomber Command Squash Trophy on a couple of occasions.

Life in the RAF involved officers on very different contracts. If you were a permanent commissioned officer, it was presumed that you were planning a full career in the RAF. If you were on a short service commission, then you might be in the RAF for say, four, eight, or twelve years. These commissions were potentially beneficial to those seeking high salaries as they would leave the RAF as trained pilots and join civilian airlines. I wrote an article entitled 'Pilot—Service or Civilian?' in which I evaluated the pay and pensions of RAF and civilian pilots. Assuming a competent civil pilot retained his medical fitness, he would retire on a pension equivalent to that of an Air Vice Marshal, whereas less than 3 per cent of pilots achieved that rank. Soon after obtaining the appointment of Valiant captain, I wrote to the British Overseas Airways Corporation requesting a job as a BOAC pilot. I went to Heathrow for an interview and was offered a job subject to three conditions:

1. That you can obtain release from the Royal Air Force
2. That you pass a BOAC medical examination
3. That your references prove satisfactory

I discussed this offer with certain friends and they advised me not to progress with it as the RAF would not release me having just completed a Valiant captain's course.

A camouflaged
Valiant.

As I mentioned above, in May my crew flew in the RAF Bombing
Competition. Strategic Air Command, which controlled the bomber force in
the US Air Force, held a bombing competition in October and the RAF was
invited to participate, so crews from RAF Marham and a crew from No. 90
Squadron, captained by John Cochrane, all flew out to California. I have a
letter from Riverside, California, dated 3 October 1958 from John, much of
which I quote:

> Contrary to all expectations, I am in fact writing this promised letter.
> Appreciate the fact that the temperature outside is 103 degrees and you'll
> know what a kind, thoughtful sod I am.
>
> No doubt rumours have filtered back about what a wonderful place this
> is, in actual truth it's much better than that but I'll be glad to get home
> for a rest. I've seldom seen so much 'ass' and never have I imagined more
> reasonable and single minded people—copulation is the national sport. Not
> that XC (90 Squadron) indulges at all, although as a squadron we've been
> famous for leading the field at every forum of extra normal activity! Excuse
> the writing but our room is in semi darkness so that Paddy can get some
> sleep before 'the ball' starts again this evening.

Now follows a short account of the professional account of this detachment—this 'organisation' being henceforward referred to as 'malfunction junction'. This outfit is the bitter end. It's been generally accepted as Marham [in big print] and the rest [in small]. My crew's performance has ranked about second or third in training out here and a few days ago we put up the second best trip of any. But we were informed that although we were good boys we would regretfully remain reserves whilst certain (Marham) squadron Leaders and Wing Commanders remained in the team. Not only my crew were disgusted at that little effort—even some of the Marham crews were! Cochrane, of course, has done more duties (extraneous) with Paddy than the rest of the crews put together. Altogether we were 'pissed off'.

Tuesday saw a big change when poor old Ken went bonkers—that put Freddie's crew out and my crew in—pity it had to be that way though. However Cochrane's boys rose to the occasion last night with five bombs under 320 metres and one mile on astro, which is emphatically the best performance of the detachment and has made the losers sit up and take notice.

I'm not giving you any information about the sex life of the American females for obvious reasons—it might get into wrong hands and would hate to be responsible for any more divorces! Take it from me—Phil you'd just do your little nut out here trying to get through it all in the time available!

Must go now. Take care of yourself and don't overdo it!

Fondest regards, Jock.

In those days we had many Scots in the RAF and let us hope that continues! As you can see, they set the very highest standards of co-operation.

As the letter above suggests, during these years we lived a very varied life with another detachment to RAF Luqa in Malta. Then in May, Princess Margaret was opening a British Exhibition at Lisbon in Portugal and No. 90 Squadron was to provide a formation display. We had four aircraft preparing but unfortunately two had technical faults, so just two aircraft set off for Lisbon. Our excellent technical officer cleared the fault in my aircraft so I took off about twenty minutes late. We flew through the London Control Zone, cut across through the north of Spain and joined the formation as they were approaching Lisbon. We made a couple of displays over Lisbon and then headed home, where we received a signal from the Prime Minister, Harold McMillan, congratulating us on our excellent performance.

In October 1958 the Norwegian Air Force invited the RAF to visit Norway to go on a winter survival course. Two pilots from Honington were selected—Freddie Scott and myself. We flew to Norway, spent a few days being briefed on winter survival and then a night in Oslo prior to our days in the cold. Everyone was well aware of the cost of alcohol in Norway, so we phoned the British Embassy and explained that some 'very poor' RAF aircrew were preparing for a survival course—they kindly supplied whisky, gin, and wine at unbelievable prices. The Norwegian aircrew supplied the food and attractive ladies and we certainly had a memorable party in Oslo. Having survived the party we set off for the cold lands of Norway where we were towed on skis behind motorized vehicles, airlifted in helicopters, and exposed to all the dangers of the harsh environment. We were given special chocolate bars to assist in our survival. I was cutting the chocolate with a sharp knife on my winter glove and the knife went through the chocolate, my glove, and my hand! Blood was everywhere. As the next most senior pilot on the course, Freddie Scott assumed command, and eventually I was flown off in a helicopter. It certainly was a memorable winter survival course.

Freddie was the son of a British executive in India, so he was educated in India and returned to the UK for his national service. He was doing his training at RAF Hednesford near Stafford. The recruits were asked what games they played and he was selected for the soccer team. One day a visiting hockey team was short of a player; having played hockey in India, Freddie volunteered to help out. The visitors won 7–1, with Freddie scoring six goals. By the end of the year he was selected to play for Scotland and in 1955 he was selected to represent the UK in the Olympic Games. In 1960, when he was a co-pilot on No. 7 Squadron, he was again selected for the Olympic Games. Apparently his squadron commander pointed out that as he was a co-pilot on a Valiant squadron he could not fulfil two duties at the same time and therefore had to make a choice. He responded by saying that it was an incredible honour to be selected for the Olympic Games and while he had no wish to leave the squadron, his priority must be to represent his country. Within half an hour he was called in by the station commander and told that he would not be leaving the squadron and a concession had been made to allow him to represent his country in the Olympic Games.

My next two years on the squadron were very similar, with routine training, detachments to Malta and Nairobi in Kenya, bombing competitions, and Battle of Britain formation displays. In June 1959 I was staying in the RAF Club in London and I thought I would read the paper to see who had been rewarded in the Queen's Honour List—lo and behold, there was the name of Flight Lieutenant P. J. Goodall awarded a Queen's Commendation for Valuable Service in the Air. When I returned to Honington, I was required to see the station commander who informed me that I had been recommended to receive an Air Force Cross and apologised that I had got second best.

In March 1960 my crew went on our first Western Ranger to the USA. One of my navigators, Russ Rumbol, wrote an account of our visit:

90 Squadron Valiants in the Far East.

St Patrick in Omaha

The Lone Ranger, to most people, is redolent of Tonto, Silver and the overture to William Tell. To some of us in the Royal Air Force, it meant a nice jolly—a flight to an interesting place abroad for a few days. The purpose was to operate and be self-dependent without the usual back-up of a permanent base. It was still a nice jolly.

A Western Ranger was one of the delights of the V-Force. We flew from our UK base to Goose Bay in Labrador. After a short stay the next stop was Offutt, no less than the Headquarters of Strategic Air Command.

Offutt was a typical American base, except that it was, as said, the Headquarters of Strategic Air Command, the epi-centre of the Western deterrent. We were shown around, but it was a public tour—not just because we were in the V-force. I was surprised by how much was revealed; I'd have thought it was mostly classified. No one could have failed to be impressed by the efficacy of the system. It might have done some good for our doubters back in the UK to see it.

Then we hit the town. Omaha, Nebraska, is about the size of Nottingham and I can remember little of the town itself except that it appeared to be deficient of toilets. That is how the fun started. It was suggested to us to make use of a bar. Inside it was obviously St Patrick's Day. Everything was green, including the beer. How horrible, we thought. Then a green pint appeared in front of each of us.

Before we could protest, the barman said, 'compliments of the gentleman down the bar.' Then advanced a small, very tough looking man, the image of James Cagney, with his hand outstretched. 'The name is O'Brian,' he announced.

Oh dear, here's trouble! We knew that many Irish Americans hated the English and especially when drinking on St Patrick's Day. Luckily there were four of us. But when we returned his greeting, he exclaimed, 'say, are you guys English?' He turned out to be a lovely chap and incredibly pro-British. He had himself been in the US Navy during the war. His father was in the IRA in the early years of the century and left for the States when things got to be too hot. In the First World War, he didn't wait for 1917 but joined the British Army, got the Military Medal and died fighting for the old enemy in Mons. His son had a similar affection and seemed to delight in our company, pressed more green beer on to us and gave us each a silver dollar. Mine is now in the custody of my grandson.

Food was clearly called for but it was not to be. The next place we made was like the previous one but more so. I don't remember sitting down to a meal but I do remember a great deal of noise and a splendid welcome. If it were not for all the green, you'd have thought it was St George's Day. We weren't able to put our hands in our pockets once.

It was election year and a fellow called Kennedy was on everyone's lips. I found this surprising for I knew that Omaha was in the mid-west, which I thought was Republican territory. But Kennedy it was, as all the costumes and beer mats said.

Just two years later, we had the Cuban crisis and the same crew were sitting in a V-bomber waiting for the call. Disaster was saved by the statesmanship of Kruschev [*sic*], Macmillan and Kennedy—not to mention the Anglo-American deterrent. Put some other names in there and who knows what would have happened.

We told tales, we sang songs and told insulting transatlantic jokes, taken in good humour on both sides. 'The Yanks are flying Fortresses at forty thousand feet but they only drop a teeny weeny bomb.' 'Yeah, you Brits will always fight to the last man—to the last American man.'

Our jokes were down to earth but not too rude because there were a good many women in the bar. A very attractive one took a shine to Brian Warwick, our tall, blond co-pilot. She likened him to Tab Hunter. At that time of course, Mr Hunter had not 'come out'; otherwise Brian would have thought it a doubtful compliment! I seemed to gravitate to the mature ones—just my luck as I was only in my twenties. To one lady I gave the benefit of my vast knowledge of American politics, from the Monroe Doctrine to the Marshall Plan. She seemed impressed and was very attentive and polite. When we left, she gave me her card (which I still have). It said 'Mimi Olsen, Democratic Chairwoman for the State of Nebraska.' What a berk, she no doubt thought.

Came leaving time and we were full of almost tearful regrets. 'Come and see us again the next time you're here.' We were in high spirits and full of bonhomie but not drunk—it was only American beer after all. In the taxi back to camp, reality set in. At 0800 the following morning, we were going to fly back. How was it possible? At Offutt, we were met by the crew chief. Our aircraft was u/s and would take at least a day to fix. We almost kissed him!

When Russ retired from the RAF he became a teacher and I guess all his students enjoyed writing.

In September 1960 I was chosen to display a Valiant in the Canadian International Air Display in Toronto. I carried out a couple of displays at base so that I was authorised to carry out the same displays in Toronto. One of the interesting events at Toronto was the reception on the Thursday evening held in the Royal York Hotel, which was apparently the largest hotel in the British Commonwealth. When we were called in to the dinner, I was asked by a journalist if I had a special seat—he then said 'Come with me'. I was sitting opposite the Russian Air Attaché and next to the runner-up in the Miss Canada Competition. The Russian Air Attaché and I had a fascinating discussion but he had his political advisor sitting next to him, who was constantly talking in Russian and seemed to be telling him to shut up.

Fortunately the air displays were a success. We then started for home via Goose Bay in Labrador. On the way to Goose Bay we had an engine failure so flew there on three engines; we had to wait for nearly three weeks for a replacement engine before finally returning to the UK. Our routine continued until February 1961, when we went on another trip to Malaya via El Adem, Nairobi, Gan on the Maldives, and into RAF Butterworth. The Maldives are now one of the most exclusive holiday destinations in the world, but in those days they hosted an RAF base. We were restricted in which islands we could visit but enjoyed listening to the wonderful singing of the locals as they got into a huge boat rowed home to their island at the end of each day. Back at RAF Honington we had the annual Bomber Command Bombing Competition which was won by our squadron, but that was the end of my tour on No. 90 Squadron. I have been writing about our overseas tours, air displays, and participating in bombing competitions, but we were part of the UK nuclear deterrent and that was the justification of our varied activities.

My crew had been together for over four years and in May 1961 we parted

Fisher ladies on the beach behind the Officers' Mess, Butterworth.

company. My navigator, Ken Hunt, was an ex-apprentice who then qualified as a navigator. He was involved in fitting the navigation equipment to the V-bombers and was awarded a Queen's Commendation for Valuable Service in the Air. When he was recommended for a permanent commission, a civil servant stated that he did not meet the required educational standards, so Ken set off on a new life. Russ Rumbol also left the RAF and became a school teacher, and our signaller Gus Allen, a highly intelligent engineer, also retired and began work as a lecturer in a technical training college.

In a pilot's flying log book, the commanding officer is required to give an assessment of the crew's performance; in May 1961 my ability as a Medium Bomber 1st pilot was 'Exceptional' with the comment, 'A most successful and productive tour of duty and now a great loss to the squadron.' I certainly enjoyed my four years on No. 90 Squadron and had the pleasure of an exceptional crew. Over fifty years later, Ken Hunt, Russ Rumbol, and I were still in contact—we enjoyed a reunion in 2014.

SUKHOI SU-9

The Sukhoi OKB (also known at the time as the OKB-51), started developing swept-wing and delta-wing fighters in accordance with the general initiative of the Soviet government dating from October 1953, which called for an accelerated development of a generation of Mach 2-capable fighter types. The delta-wing T-3 prototype made its maiden flight on 26 May 1956.

The first T-43 delta-wing prototype, built on the T-3 base, powered by the AL-7F-1, and provided with a new nose section with a two-position centre body shock-cone (full forward at Mach 1.35 and above and full aft at lower speeds), was flown for the first time on 10 October 1957 with Vladimir Ilyshin in the cockpit. During the third test flight on 30 October, he hit 21,500 m (70,520 feet), and three days later attained a maximum speed of 2,200 kph (1,187 kt), equating to Mach 2.06.

The T-43 was equipped with the TsD-30 radar, designed to detect and track air targets and also provide guidance for the K-5M (RS-2US) beam-riding air-to-air missile. The radar was small enough to accommodate inside the limited space available in the nose.

The two phases of the state test programme included 407 sorties, and the effort was officially completed on 9 April 1960. The test completion report noted that all basic characteristics set out in the government decree had been achieved. The air-intercept system was able to destroy air targets flying at speeds between 800 and 1,600 kph (431 and 863 kt), and at altitudes between 5,000 and 20,000 m (16,400 and 65,600 feet); the probability of target destruction was found to be between 0.7 and 0.9, while the maximum intercept radius was 430 km (232 nm).

The T-43 was formally commissioned in Soviet Air Defence Forces service on 15 October 1960, receiving the Su-9 (NATO reporting name 'Fishpot-A') designation, while the radar was designated as the RP-9U and the missile as the RS-2US. The overall air-intercept system was designated as the Su-9-51. The new aircraft was shown in public for the first time during the 9 July 1961 parade in Tushino.

The series production of the Su-9 was launched immediately after the completion of the factory testing in 1958 and the new type was rolled out at the GAZ-153 plant in Novosibirsk until 1962. In parallel with the Novosibirsk production line, it was also launched in production at the GAZ-30 in Moscow, with the first two pre-series examples rolled out in mid-1959. The full-scale series production was launched in 1960 and continued until 1961. The total production run at the two plants accounted for 888 single-seat and 126 two-seat aircraft.

Sukhoi Su-9 fighter.

During the improvement process, the Su-9 received a strengthened armament with the K-55 heat-seeking missiles, an RS-2US derivative fitted with an IR seeker borrowed from the K-13 (R-3S) missile. The tests proved to be very protracted due to problems encountered with the new missile, and were completed in 1967. The new missile was commissioned in service under the R-55 designation, and the improved radar, capable of providing targeting and launch information, was designated as the RP-9UK.

In 1966–67, two production-standard Su-9s were used in a programme to test bomb employment, mainly involving the FAB-250 250-kg (550-lb) high-explosive bombs. In the late 1960s the aircraft was tested with the UPK-23-250 gun-pods, installed under the fuselage, using the pylons previously occupied by external fuel tanks. The results from the UPK-23-250 tests were promising but it was not used in the front-line units because without external tanks the Su-9 suffered from a shortened range.

The Su-9 proved to be a brand-new reality for the IA PVO in the early 1960s as it was much more complex and effective than the previous fighter types operated by the service, such as the MiG-15, MiG-17, and MiG-19P/PM.

By the mid-1960s, the Su-9 was operated by no fewer than thirty IA PVO regiments. Its induction-into-service period between 1961 and

1963 saw a very high attrition rate, with most of the accidents caused by the engine (mostly due to failures in the automatic compressor control and the fuel system), electrical system, and hydraulic booster failures. A significant proportion of the accidents were attributed to pilot and technical mistakes as it was a complex aircraft with many systems that needed skilled operation and servicing.

The combat training syllabus required Su-9 pilots to master several typical intercept profiles comprising of attacks on low-speed/high-altitude targets (such as the U-2), medium-altitude/subsonic targets (such as the B-47 and B-52 heavy bombers), and high-altitude/high-speed small-sized targets (such as the AGM-28 Hound Dog cruise missile). The list of the practice targets used in these intercept training missions included the Yak-25RV (to simulate the U-2), the Tu-16 (to replicate the US subsonic bombers), and Su-9 itself (set to replicate the AGM-28 Hound Dog). The most difficult typical intercept was that performed against the U-2 or similar high-altitude targets, flying at 500 to 600 kph (270 to 324 kt) at the Su-9's operational ceiling. The interceptor was required to initially climb to the base altitude of about 10,000 m (32,800 feet), to accelerate to Mach 1.6 in level flight, and then enter in climb, maintaining an instrument speed no lower than 1,100 kph (593 kt), equating to Mach 1.9 at altitudes near the practical ceiling. In fact, the pilot had to maintain no lower than Mach 1.7 since at lower speeds the Su-9 was not able to maintain level flight. At the same time, the pilot was tasked to follow the guidance instructions from the ground intercept control officer; the intercept was performing in a limited timeframe because the closure speed between the interceptor and the target was too high.

In the late 1960s, the Su-9 became an effective interceptor with trained crews and a reliable mission avionics suite.

8

No. 7 Squadron—Valiant Flight Commander

In June 1961 I was promoted to Squadron Leader and posted as a flight commander to No. 7 Squadron, based at RAF Wittering, near Stamford in Lincolnshire. At this time most RAF personnel lived in married quarters which were normally located on the RAF base. We were allocated a married quarter on a points system, which meant the longer you had been married, the more points you earned. As I was not married until the age of twenty-nine, I had never lived in a married quarter, but as a flight commander on No. 7 Valiant Squadron, I was now allowed this privilege and was allocated a house. As the RAF had built a quantity of new houses on Boxer Road, my wife and I went up to inspect our new home. It was an ideal house with all the facilities, but I informed the admin branch responsible for the married quarters that I could not get the electricity to work. The officer responsible duly arrived to show this 'new occupant' the simple means of switching on the electricity. However, he failed, and further inspection revealed that a new road of houses had been built, but electricity had not been connected to any of them. By the time we moved in, we fortunately had power.

When I joined No. 7 Squadron, my new crew had also relocated from Honington and I knew all the members, including my new navigator, Terry Hoare, who had been Best Man at my wedding. We immediately resumed flying with exercises and operations, identical to my years at Honington. During my operational service in the RAF, all my squadron commanders had been pilots, but joining No. 7 Squadron was a change as it was commanded by Wing Commander Jack Wilson, a navigator. I wondered if there would be any differences.

During my years flying in the V-Force we used to receive an 'Aircrew Classification Certificate' with either a 'Select' or 'Select Star' classification; the award of these classifications enabled crews to have trips overseas. When I joined No. 7 Squadron, my crew had a 'Select Star' classification which meant that we would fly on Lone Rangers or Western Rangers to the United States. In October 1961 we were off on a Lone Ranger to Idris Airport in Libya, and the next day flew to Nairobi in Kenya.

When RAF crews flew to Nairobi we used to contact the hospital and invite the nurses out for a drink. I believe this was an interesting social gathering for both groups, but it would seem that the popularity of the RAF increased the 'contacts' in Nairobi. On Friday we would fly down to Salisbury and spend a weekend enjoying the sights in Rhodesia, then on the Monday morning we would return to Nairobi. Early on Monday morning I received a phone call from my crew chief, who was in an awful state:

> Sir, I am happily married. On Thursday evening I was enjoying the social gathering when a lady invited me home for a drink. I had no idea that she expected me to sleep with her and at 7.00 on Friday morning her staff arrived with a cup of tea. Apparently she is the wife of a Colonel. I think I have caught VD.

I suggested that it was too soon to identify any medical problem, but arranged for him to see a doctor, who gave him the all clear. When we arrived in Nairobi we had a queue of friends but all decided to prepare for an early return. On Tuesday we flew to El Adem in Libya and home on Wednesday.

I was recounting this story to a friend and he had memories of a similar trip. When his crew arrived in Salisbury, they were informed that the black navigator could not sleep in the Officers' Mess. The captain responded by saying that the crew would therefore make an immediate return to Nairobi. After reconsideration, the captain was informed that the black navigator could spend the weekend in the Officers' Mess; when they left on the Monday, the mattress, sheets, and blankets of the black navigator were all taken out and burnt.

This account of our activities is being written in the twenty-first century, thus certain names need to be changed. Nairobi in Kenya is still known by its old name, but Salisbury in Southern Rhodesia is now Harare in Zimbabwe. I doubt if the twenty-first century RAF makes regular trips into Zimbabwe.

In December we had another dispersal exercise—'Kinsman'—and my crew flew to RAF Lyneham in Wiltshire. The C-in-C of Bomber Command, Air Marshal Sir Kenneth Cross, would fly to the dispersal airfields to ensure that the plans were professionally implemented. I showed him around the dispersal and he asked me if I had any problems and I responded by saying 'No major problems'. 'What are your minor problems?' he replied. I explained that we were supposed to have Land Rovers so that we could move all the ground equipment, but only one had been delivered. He instructed his personal assistant to investigate and the next morning the Land Rovers were miraculously delivered. By the end of the week the exercise was successfully completed and we flew back to base. My squadron commander asked if the exercise had been successful and I confirmed that we had met all our operational requirements. He commented that I had apparently made a complaint to the C-in-C, who had then demanded an explanation on the missing Land Rovers by 6.00 a.m. the following morning, and I was informed that many high ranking officers had been up half the night trying to arrange for the delivery of the vehicles. Apparently efficiency is more important than popularity!

Life on No. 7 Squadron was very similar to the activities at Honington: commitment to the UK nuclear deterrent with targets for all crews, bombing exercises, Western Rangers to Goose Bay in Labrador and to Offutt in Nebraska, participation in bombing competitions, and Western Rangers to Nairobi and Salisbury in Rhodesia.

October 1962 was the time of the Cuban Missile Crisis, when a U-2 aircraft produced photographic evidence of medium-range and intermediate-range ballistic nuclear weapons sites in Cuba. The USA initiated a military blockade of Cuba and demanded dismantlement and a return of the Soviet weapons back to the USSR. Confrontation ended on 28 October when President Kennedy and the UN Secretary General reached an agreement with Nikita Khrushchev. Interestingly, a Washington–Moscow hotline was established. Fortunately the USA, Russia, and the United Nations were able to agree and mutual destruction was avoided; a lesson to be remembered.

Just fourteen months after I was appointed as a flight commander on No. 7 Squadron, we were informed that the squadron was being closed down. On 22 October I flew the last Valiant from Wittering. Just eight years before it had been the first operational V-bomber base in the UK. In fact, No. 138 Squadron, the first 'V' Squadron, had been disbanded on 1 April 1962. Structural problems on the Valiant were first diagnosed following a flight from Gaydon in August 1964, when engineers found that the rear spar in the starboard mainplane was cracked. Following exhaustive tests it was decided on 27 January 1965 that the Valiant would be withdrawn from service. There had been seven Valiant squadrons, of which No. 543, based at RAF Wyton, specialised in photographic reconnaissance. As a result of the Valiant's structural problems, the squadron was re-equipped with Victors during 1965 and disbanded on 24 May 1974.

No. 49 Squadron, flying the Vickers Valiant, was tasked with dropping the British nuclear weapons. Operation Buffalo detailed plans for release of the first nuclear weapon at Maralinga in South Australia on 11 October 1956. Operation Grapple resulted in the RAF dropping two nuclear weapons in the megaton range at Christmas Island in the Pacific in May 1957, with a third in June 1957. Trials continued with various scientific tests, then in mid-1959 the decision was taken by Prime Minister Harold Macmillan that the UK would carry out no further nuclear tests. No. 49 Squadron was finally disbanded on 1 May 1965. The remaining Valiant squadrons were all disbanded—No. 214

at Marham on 28 February 1965, and Nos 207 and 148 Squadrons, both also based at Marham, on 28 April 1965. It was the end of the Valiant force. The sole remaining Vickers Valiant (XD818)—the aircraft that dropped the first British hydrogen bomb at Christmas Island with No. 49 Squadron as part of Operation Grapple—is preserved at the RAF Museum Cosford, near Wolverhampton.

When I think about the first four-engine jet bomber to enter RAF service, an aircraft of fascinating design and the only RAF aircraft to drop nuclear weapons, I question why there is only one aircraft still in existence. Do we blame senior RAF officer or the civil service? Fortunately someone saw sense and there are still many Vulcans, and even one still flying in 2015, but in my view, the destruction of the Valiants was a military and political disgrace.

The disbandment of No. 7 Squadron meant that all personnel would be involved in new duties. I was selected to go to the RAF Staff College in January 1963, which was based at Bracknell in Berkshire. My fellow flight commander

Five Vulcans at dispersal, painted in anti-flash white.

was posted to Singapore, and my squadron commander, Wing Commander Jack Wilson, was posted to the Ministry of Defence (MoD) to work in the personnel department.

In July 1969 I was selected to attend the RAF Air Warfare Course, which was at RAF Manby, and my former Valiant commanding officer was on the same course. He told me that he had given both his flight commanders excellent reports. When he was in the personnel department at the MoD, he examined the reports from pilots in Fighter Command and realised that they were given 'walk on water' assessments to ensure that pilots of Fighter Command controlled the RAF. Following his tour in Singapore, my former associate retired from the RAF and in months was an airline captain. I wonder if my former squadron commander examined the personal assessments of former apprentices who entered the RAF College as cadets? If the RAF is to fulfil its military commitment to the United Kingdom, it needs to have senior officers appointed on their abilities rather than their background.

AVRO VULCAN

Avro was one of six British aircraft manufacturers to receive 'Specification B.35/46' in January 1947 from the Ministry of Supply. The document requested designs for 'a medium-range bomber landplane capable of carrying one 10,000-lb bomb to a target 1,500 nautical miles from a base which may be anywhere in the world'. The aircraft needed to be capable of cruising at 575 mph and reaching an altitude of 50,000 feet. This was the specification to move the RAF into a new age of high sub-sonic flight with jet bombers able to fly at speeds and altitudes beyond the reach of fighters. With this technology, the British Government would harness the ultimate deterrent to attack in the post-war era—the nuclear bomb.

The Avro design team recognised at once that a conventional aircraft would not meet the demands of the specification. It seemed that the British aviation industry was lagging in the race for technological supremacy, as was the USA. Germany, however, had made considerable advances in 'swept-wing' research during the Second World War, and it was German delta-winged designs that provided Avro with the foundation from which to explore the possibilities of high-speed flight.

Avro's technical director Roy Chadwick and chief designer Stuart Davies drew upon the visionary work of Prof. Alexander Lippisch who had pioneered the delta-wing design and experimented with supersonic flight under the direction of the Reich Air Ministry throughout the war.

They developed Lippisch's ideas and moulded them into a design that tested the limits of aeronautical technology.

The initial Avro submission was for a tailless delta-wing aircraft powered by four turbojet engines—two within each wing—with outboard bomb bays and wingtip fins for stability. Following Roy Chadwick's tragic death on a test flight of the Avro Tudor 2 prototype airliner in August 1947, Stuart Davies was teamed with Sir William Farren. Under this new partnership some modifications were made to the initial design: the thickness of the wings was reduced, a single bomb bay was placed between the pairs of turbojets with 'letter box' inlets, and the wingtip fins were scrapped in favour of a single fin along the aircraft's centreline. In January 1948, the Avro team received the go-ahead to construct two prototypes of their design, known as Avro Type 698.

Simultaneous to the construction of the Type 698, Avro decided to build two smaller prototypes to gain much-needed flight experience of the new delta-wing design. Avro Type 707 was designed as a one-third-scale model of the 698 to test the aircraft's handling at low speed, and Avro Type 710 as a half-scale model to test handling at high speed. The latter was soon cancelled as it demanded excessive time and expense, and the one-third-scale high-speed 707A was built in its place. Tragically, the first prototype crashed in September 1949, less than a month after its debut flight, killing the test pilot. Further delays and difficulties with the 707 programme meant that it contributed little to the development of the Avro 698.

The first Rolls-Royce Avon-powered Avro Type 698 prototype (serial VX770), with a pure-delta planform, was ready to fly in August 1952. Apart from the undercarriage doors coming loose and falling from the aircraft mid-flight, the test flight was a success. A year later, in September 1953, a second prototype (serial VX 777) of the newly named 'Vulcan' was taken to the air, this time fitted with Bristol Siddeley Olympus 104 engines, a crucial part of the initial design which would enable the Vulcan to achieve its full potential. However, the added power of the engines meant that the aircraft experienced severe instability during high-speed manoeuvres and, when approaching supersonic speeds, tended to enter an uncontrollable dive. Davies and Farren overcame this problem by redesigning the wing to have a kinked and dropped leading edge.

In May 1957 the first Vulcan squadron—No. 83 at RAF Waddington, Lincolnshire—was formed, equipped with the all-white anti-flash Vulcan B.1 with 58-inch toned-down RAF roundel. At this time the threat posed by Soviet Russia was becoming increasingly apparent, and overall

Ground crew working on a Vulcan Mk2, XM570, fitted with a Blue Steel missile.

Crew waiting to board a 27 Squadron Vulcan Mk2.

White Vulcan Mk1s based at Waddington.

defensive strategy was becoming more dependent on technological advances. 1957 also saw the publication of the 'White Paper on Defence', which outlined the government's plans to reduce the size of the British Army and invest in aircraft capable of operating in the new 'missile age'.

The Vulcan B.1 had been designed to have the speed and ceiling to make it invulnerable to enemy attack, but with the emergence of the guided missile and surface-to-air missile, no aircraft could claim to be invulnerable. A vast overhaul of the B.1 design was required to give pilots a greater chance of success (and survival) if called upon to carry out a nuclear attack on the USSR. While the Avro Blue Steel 'standoff' nuclear missile was being developed, so too were more sophisticated electronic countermeasures (ECM) to protect the V-bombers from Soviet defences.

White Vulcans on dispersal base at the end of the runway.

In the new Vulcan B.2, the latest ECM equipment was contained in a large bulge behind its tail, the wing area was increased and given its distinctive aerodynamic curvature, the engines were upgraded to a more powerful version of the Rolls-Royce Olympus, and the air intakes in the wings were deepened in anticipation of future engines with an even greater capacity. The B.2 was also specially designed to carry the 'Blue Steel' nuclear missile—then under development—and first entered service in 1960 with No. 83 Squadron, like its predecessor, B.1.

In 1963, after the introduction of the Avro Blue Steel standoff missile, improvements to the Soviet SAM system and fighter defences forced the RAF to review its strategy of high-altitude bombing. A technique known as 'lob-bombing' was adopted whereby Blue Steel was launched about

A Vulcan Mk 2 landing.

A white Vulcan with Blue Steel.

100 miles from the target at 50,000 feet, with the release point fixed by the Vulcan's NBS radar. After launch the missile climbed to 59,000 feet, and four minutes after release, dived onto the target from an altitude of 71,000 feet, with the V-bomber well on its way home. However, flying at high altitudes offered no defence against the Soviet surface-to-air missiles, but flying close to the ground decreased the chances of radar detection—a distinct advantage, despite lowering the aircraft's fatigue life. The change in strategy to low-level operations was marked by a change in livery for the Vulcan: the standard white 'anti-flash' finish was replaced by a dark green and grey disruptive pattern on the upper surface to reduce detection from above. The following year, V-Force reached its peak: the RAF boasted a total of 159 V-bombers, with 70 Avro Vulcans, 50 Vickers Valiants, and 39 Handley Page Victors.

Although each Vulcan cost over £1 million to build—a considerable fortune in the 1960s—it was universally hoped that it would never be

A Vulcan B2 at RAF Scampton.

A 90 Squadron Valiant at RAF Honington.

Vulcan B2 at Davis Monthan Air Force Base in the US.

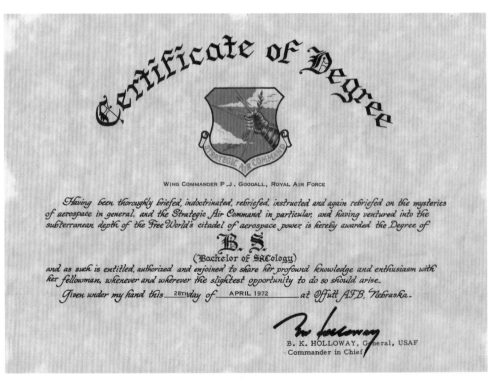

Certificate of Degree for Wing Commander P. J. Goodall, presented by General Holloway, the C-in-C of SAC.

90 Squadron Valiant crew: PJG, Brian Warwick, Gus Allen, Russ Rumbol, and Ken Hunt.

90 Squadron Valiant crew with the Crew Chief on the far right.

Left: Valiant Captain—PJG.

Below: 90 Squadron Valiant crew: Flight Lieutenant Warwick (co-pilot), PJG (captain), Flight Lieutenant Ken Hunt (navigator plotter), Master Signaller Gus Allen (signaller), Flight Lieutenant Russ Rumbol (navigator radar), April 1958.

Welcome to the 1971 SAC Bombing Competition.

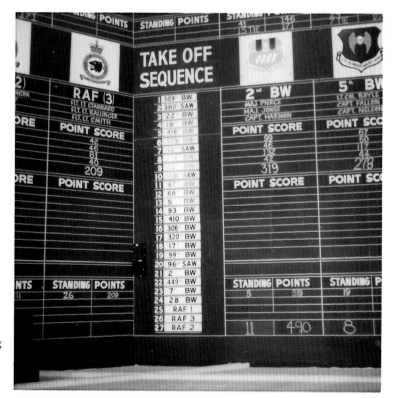

SAC Bombing Competition take off sequences.

A 90 Squadron Valiant at RAF Honington.

Flight Lieutenant Brian Warwick, co-pilot in a 90 Squadron Valiant.

A Vulcan leading a formation at Farnborough Air Show, 1958.

90 Squadron Valiants in formation.

An airborne view of a white Victor.

An airborne view of a white Vulcan.

Vulcans and a Victor at Goose Bay, Labrador, during the winter.

A 90 Squadron Valiant at RAF Honington.

Vulcan Mk2 at Davis Monthan Air Force Base, Arizona, in March 1968.

A B52 with missiles at Davis Monthan Air Force Base in Arizona.

A Vulcan Mk2 with Blue Steel at Offutt Air Force Base in Nebraska.

An aerial photograph of a Vulcan B2.

A 90 Squadron Valiant in the Far East.

An Avro Lancaster at RAF Scampton for the Stand-Down of Bomber Command on 29 April 1968.

A Victor Mk2 on the ground at an air display.

A Vulcan in a steep climb.

A Valiant at RAF Honington.

A Vulcan Mk2 fitted with a Blue Steel missile.

A Vulcan Mk2 with other aircraft at Davis Monthan.

A Vulcan Mk1 painted anti-flash white at RAF Waddington.

A white Victor Mk1.

In the 90 Squadron detachment to the Far East in April 1958, my crew had no aircraft for three weeks, so I had the pleasure of being a co-pilot and flying a Hastings to Hong Kong and back.

Vulcan
Mk2 XM51
being
serviced.

Crew
preparing
to leave in a
Vulcan Mk2
fitted with
Blue Steel.

Crew
leaving
Vulcan
Mk2 with
Blue Steel.

Crew
entering 27
Squadron
Vulcan
Mk2 fitted
with Blue
Steel.

called upon to carry out its primary role—an attack on Soviet Russia with nuclear weapons. As with the other two V-bombers, the Vulcan was a part of the UK's nuclear deterrent programme to safeguard against the threat of a Soviet strike on Great Britain. In 1968, with the introduction of the Polaris nuclear submarine programme, this role diminished. However, the Vulcan was also designed to carry out conventional bombing sorties with a maximum of twenty-one 1,000-lb HE bombs, and it was in this capacity that it saw action during the Falklands War in 1982.

By the early 1980s, the Vulcan was soon to be retired from active service—only three RAF squadrons (Nos 44, 50, and 101) were still equipped with the aircraft and just five aircraft were suitable for long-distance bombing sorties. On 30 April Vulcan XM607 flew a 16-hour sortie from RAF Ascension Island in the middle of the South Atlantic Ocean to Port Stanley, the capital of the Falkland Islands, where twenty-one 1,000-lb HE bombs were dropped on the airport runway. This was the longest bombing sortie in the history of aviation warfare to date, and XM607 required ten Handley Page Victor tankers for air-to-air refuelling during the flight. A further four Vulcan bombing sorties, known collectively as the 'Black Buck' raids, were carried out on military targets on the Falkland Islands in May and early June. Although the damage caused was limited, the Black Buck raids had a considerable psychological effect, demonstrated by the withdrawal of some Mirage III/ and Mirage VA 'Dagger' fighter jets to defend against the possibility of an attack on the Argentinian mainland. No Vulcans were shot down, although one, XM597, was forced to land on 1 June in neutral Brazil after the breaking of its refuelling probe. The aircraft and its crew were detained in custody until 10 June.

In March 1984, two years after the Falklands War, the last Vulcan squadron, No. 50, with six K.2 in-flight refueller conversion aircraft and air show demonstration aircraft XH558, was disbanded. Many were scrapped or used as fire practice airframes, while some were bought and preserved by museums and private enthusiasts. One aircraft, XH558, was retained by the RAF in operational condition for display purposes until 1993, when the MoD ruled that it could no longer afford to keep it airworthy. XH558 is now owned by the 'Vulcan to the Sky Trust' and has been restored to flight display condition.

The Avro Vulcan is one of the most iconic aircraft of the Cold War period, representing the pinnacle of post-war design and technology. Its twenty-eight years of front-line operational service in the RAF are testament to its advanced design and enduring value as part of the RAF's Cold War bomber fleet.

A Vulcan
Mk2 on
take off,
probably
at RAF
Scampton.

Rear
view of
a Vulcan
Mk2
carrying a
Blue Steel
missile.

9

RAF Staff College and Headquarters Bomber Command

In January 1963 I was posted to the RAF Staff College at Bracknell in Berkshire. The course comprised about ninety officers for staff training and included officers from the Army, Navy, and the United States Air Force. There were many married quarters on the base which were occupied by both the staff and students. The year was similar to an educational establishment with an Easter break and summer holiday of about a month. We were split into groups of about ten with an officer monitoring his pupils, and were required to write reports on numerous subjects with questions such as, 'A fighter squadron is to be formed. Evaluate which airfield is the most suitable and cost effective.'

I also sensed that there was indoctrination to explain the politics of the country together with an explanation of the importance of the Royal Family and the House of Lords. We obviously had presentations from senior officers of the three services with the intention of instigating intelligent military understanding. I recall that King Hussein I of Jordan visited the college and gave a fascinating talk about the Middle East. King Hussein had been educated at Harrow and the Royal Military Academy at Sandhurst and one of his former RAF staff officers was on the course. The security during the visit was akin to the security at military bases today, and I recall that his former RAF aide always wore a loose double-breasted suit as he had a revolver under his left arm.

Every student was required to give a presentation of about one hour. A cousin of mine, Professor Frank George, was on the staff at Brunel University and he provided me with a teaching machine which enabled me to give a talk on computers. Interestingly, he had served as a pilot during the war which enabled him to go to Cambridge University and enter the world of cybernetics, which is described in *Automation, Cybernetics and Society* by Dr Frank George as 'the science of control and communications in animals and machines'. It sounds as if it should be a compulsory course for all politicians.

We also had the advantage of many sports facilities such as a rugby pitch and tennis and squash courts. I was very light for my height and decided I should train to be a rugby referee—the only rugby match ever won by the Staff College was when I was the referee! The College also had a team which participated with many local tennis clubs and our commandant was an effective participant. I mention this as I played tennis and squash in representative teams for many years and was friends with a very fine tennis player. An airman accused him of making a sexual advance and he was told to resign or he would be court martialled. He resigned and I believe he was married to a young lady within a few months. Throughout my RAF service homosexuality was illegal; as it could be a means of blackmailing those who were of that inclination, it was an issue that was professionally monitored. As I worked as part of the UK nuclear deterrent, we were regularly interviewed by a team of senior officers. The law in the UK has now been changed, but in many parts of the world homosexuality is still illegal.

At the Staff College we had a four-week holiday every summer to coincide with the schools. One year Steve King, a contemporary of my days at the RAF College, and I agreed that we would both grow a beard over the holiday and on return the best beard would win the bet. Steve was dark-haired and his beard was far superior to mine. At the first lecture of the new term, Steve appeared in the uniform of a naval commander with his beard and informed all that he had been promoted and transferred to the Royal Navy. There was total disbelief with everyone wondering if the services had changed their management, but then the penny dropped.

I thoroughly enjoyed my year at Staff College and understood the requirement to have officers who can write and present their views of military importance. In total contrast, just examine the background of politicians with military responsibilities and I submit that they have little understanding of the impact of the decisions they are making. For example, I suggest that Labour Party politicians would support the building of aircraft carriers because they are manufactured in Labour constituencies and thereby ensure work for their constituents. This would seem to be the deciding factor on whether or not to build aircraft carriers. In 2015 we have two aircraft carriers under construction but I am not aware of any British aircraft suitable for operation from aircraft carriers. With the present level of military strength and importance, in which part of the world would the Royal Navy operate aircraft carriers?

The RAF Staff College had been formed after the Second World War with the excellent facilities at Bracknell. With the ever reducing strength of the military, the College was closed in January 1997 when the three services formed a College at Shrivenham near Swindon in Wiltshire.

At the end of the course, three students were posted to the Headquarters of Bomber Command at RAF High Wycombe—myself, Squadron Leader Alastair Christie, and Major Richard Cody of the US Air Force, who was a graduate of West Point, the American Military Academy.

In January 1964, I joined the Air Staff with responsibility for overseas support. Having just left the Staff College, we all thought that briefings from those above would be very similar to our college training. We expected to receive a file with the appropriate correspondence and a Minute Sheet which would probably include instructions. Historically a file was identified as having a security identification and the contents would meet that requirement. The contents would be filed on the right, with a 'Minute Sheet' on the left where the person sending the file could issue instructions relating to the enclosed correspondence. They were a most efficient method of passing information and instructions. My first file came directly from the Senior Air Staff Officer, Air Vice Marshal Menaul, with a comment about another Air Marshal, 'What this idiot knows about the deterrent can be written on the back of a postage stamp. NO.' I could not recall minutes like that when I was at the Staff College. A few weeks later I heard Air Vice Marshal Menaul coming down the corridor: 'Where is that bloody man Goodall? Did you write that? So you as a Squadron Leader have taken over my responsibilities as an Air Marshal? You write the draft and forward it to me and I make the decisions, understood?'

Later I received a telephone call to report to the Air Marshal immediately—I wondered what I had done wrong this time. He handed me a letter in which he had been asked to write an article about Bomber Command. 'You are going to write this article, which I will approve.' I quote the article that was published in April 1965. When I now read what I wrote nearly fifty years ago, I realise that such articles can only be written by those living the experience.

A Day in the Life of a 'V' Bomber Pilot

With an automatic gesture I stretched out my hand to stop the incessant ringing of the alarm. I can't sneak many extra minutes this morning as I've got a long day ahead. From 8.30 until 10.00 I have a simulator trip. I think I'll put the co-pilot in the left hand seat today so he can practice the let-down procedures at Goose Bay and Offutt prior to our trip to the States next week. Then I'm due to take-off at 14.00 to take two co-pilots for their Instrument Ratings. They should both pass without too much trouble. The first has been on the squadron for two years and is due his captain's course soon; he should make a good captain with a little more experience. The other has just arrived from Cranwell. He's a very keen young man so I think I'll put him through his paces. Then this evening we've got a squash match. Lucky it is at home, as I shall be able to have a break after I land. Funny thing, I never play so well after I have been flying. I wonder why?

I was just beginning to realise that the ringing hadn't stopped when in the background I hear the tannoys blaring 'Exercise BUFFALO Exercise BUFFALO'! It's only ten minutes to three. 'Daddy! Daddy! What's that noise?' Blast! Now the kids are awake. I stumbled out of bed, 'persuade' the children to go back to sleep, get dressed and throw some things into an overnight bag. 'See you sometime darling. Better cancel that dinner tomorrow evening ... probably see you Thursday or Friday.'

I arrive at the Operations Centre, guarded, with the Police checking Identity Cards. After close scrutiny I am allowed in. The rush has now started, with aircrew arriving half dazed and in various forms of dress. I 'sign in' on the readiness board and check my crew: three more still to come. Most of the squadron have arrived, which is not bad since it is only ten minutes since the alert was called.

Exercise 'BUFFALO' is a major exercise of Bomber Command which includes everyone including the crews and aircraft already on continuous alert, or QRA, as we say. The whole Command, including the Operational Conversion Unit, practices the procedures necessary to launch the force in the retaliatory role. Other Commands in the Royal Air Force assist by providing manpower, mainly for the dispersal bases, and, of course transport aircraft, as the ground personnel for the distant dispersals are all flown in.

It is not surprising therefore that the Operations Centre is a hive of activity as this is the nerve centre of the Station's generation plan. The Technical Cell keeps a running record of the serviceability state of the aircraft and the progress of preparing them for war missions.

After 20 minutes all my crew have arrived. The Air Electronics officer was last, with his usual string of excuses, not because he was late but merely because he was last! We all change and collect our target 'GO bag', ensuring that everything is included. While waiting for the order to disperse and the final preparation of my aircraft, we go to the aircrew buffet for breakfast. It's amazing the huge meal we all eat at 3.00 in the morning; eggs, sausages, bacon, tomatoes and piles of toast. I wonder how we could possibly have existed until 7.30?

Suitably nourished we check the weather and the serviceability of the let down aids at the dispersal base; we are ready to go and await our call. Since I am the Detachment Commander, I will take the first dispersing aircraft. However, certain crews remaining at the home station have a higher priority, which means they will be allocated the first aircraft which comes available. This slight delay will allow the ground personnel for the dispersal base to be uplifted and to prepare for our arrival.

Very soon we are allocated an aircraft, the tannoy bellows my name; we're off. We grab our flying kit and hand baggage and are driven out to the aircraft to be met by a cheerful crew chief, who will fly to the dispersal with us. Rapidly we complete our checks and are soon airborne. After obtaining clearance through the airways to save time, we carry out an ILS at our dispersal base and land. I taxi around and park at the Bomber Command

Operational Readiness Platform. By the time the ground crews have arrived and are busy activating all the facilities, everything from refuelling my aircraft (The Crew Chief has already had a row over the bowsers—'They said to me "Who do you think you are, arriving this time of the day", and I said, "Bomber Command, mate"') to opening the tins of beans and arranging the delivery of fresh milk and bread, and the newspapers!

Whilst our aircraft is being serviced and refuelled we settle into our five-berth caravans which are parked a few yards from the aircraft. These will be our accommodation for the next few days. With their bunk beds, electric radiators and built-in wash basins, they are most comfortable, as they rightly should be.

The co-pilot returns to the aircraft to check the state whilst I inspect the dispersal. Meanwhile the navigators and the Air Electronics officer correct the route plan for the latest meteorological information. The dispersal accommodation is all shipshape and in good condition, as I expected. The ground crew are still positioning the ground equipment, which was naturally all serviceable as it is regularly serviced by a maintenance party. The cooks are hard at work; tea and biscuits have already been served and brunch will be available for the ground crew in half an hour. The telephones and the link to Bomber Command are all working. The teleprinter is not yet available as the operators from another Command have not yet arrived. However, there is a queer looking antiquated aircraft in the circuit which probably has them on board. I check with base; the second aircraft is airborne and the others should be off within the hour.

I return to the aircraft as the servicing has just been completed. We run through all the checks and leave the aircraft 'Cockpit Ready'. This means that when power is switched on the aircraft is immediately ready for engine start. As we are on normal readiness we can leave the aircraft. This seems a good opportunity to have the shave I missed a few hours ago.

Soon all the aircraft have arrived. They have all been refuelled and serviced and our readiness reported to Bomber Command. We had a little trouble with one aircraft but fortunately the spares backing meant the aircraft was unserviceable for a very short time. The ground crew have all eaten and have been split into their various shifts leaving starting parties at each aircraft. The aircrew have settled in; the latest planning winds and met information has been passed through from Bomber Command; we are ready.

A wholesome lunch passes uneventfully. The rosters are all drawn up. Duty Met ... Duty Officer ... and it is my turn to carry the 'GO Bag'. Wheee.... The siren blasts. We all dash madly to the aircraft. I get in first as I have to start the engines, but there is no panic as we are only being brought to cockpit readiness.

I put on my helmet and hear the 'Bleep Bleep' of Bomber Command coming over the radio, which means we are in direct contact with the

Bomber Controller. We all strap in and wait. 5–10–25–45–70 minutes pass. It's alright for those chaps in the back, they can move around but my ... is already getting sore.

This is the Bomber Controller....

Are we going? My finger is on the starting button.

Revert to normal readiness, I say again....

Just another practice.

We return to the dispersal mess and that excellent Sergeant Cook has already a mixed grill ready for us. The papers have arrived and the bridge school has formed. We will probably be here for three or four days, possibly less, with luck. The quiet mutterings of the card-players are suddenly broken by an explosion from my navigator: 'Just look at this! Why the hell don't those flaming reporters make a little effort to get their facts right.'

He has just found the article on the deterrent that I passed to him. If it was only the daily comics which misrepresented the truth it would not be too bad, but the informed press seem to do even more damage. For example, how many people know that out of a total Defence Budget of approximately £1,850 millions only £110 millions is spent on the operation of Bomber Command. The country has never had such good value for its money. One could almost coin a phrase: 'Never has so much nonsense been said by so many about so few, from whom so much is owed and from whom so little is heard.'

Well, I didn't play squash and I'm miles from home for the next few days. But it worked well today as it will always work. The aircraft were all serviced, armed and dispersed as planned. We are here and ready to go. I believe that my being here means that my children and all other children have a better chance of leading the life they want to. I know we can do what we have been trained to do, but I pray and believe we will never have to do it. Wheee...... Oh hell! Here we go again. I'll curse ... but I believe in what I'm doing.

LIFE AT THE HEADQUARTERS OF BOMBER COMMAND

The original specification for the V-bombers was that they were to be 'for world-wide use in the Royal Air Force'. An Exercise Profiteer outlined plans for V-Force detachments to the Far East. For example, Bomber Command's Operation Order 34/57 of October 1957 stated that 'two Valiant aircraft, three aircrews and ground servicing personnel will be detached to FEAF from 4 March 1958'. My crew had the pleasure of spending a month in Singapore in 1958. With the numerous V-Force detachments, my crew then spent nearly four weeks in Malaya in 1961, but now at Bomber Command

I was involved with the plans for the reinforcement of the Far East due to the friction between Malaya and Indonesia. The many Vulcan, Victor and Valiant reinforcement operations to the Far East came to an end 'following the signing of the Bangkok agreement by Malaysia and Indonesia, ending the confrontation between the two countries.'

Fortunately we also enjoyed a social life at Bomber Command. On one Sunday, three families were discussing getting tickets for the Royal Ballet in London. In those days Rudolf Nureyev and Margot Fonteyn were internationally renowned and everyone, even those with no knowledge of ballet, decided that they would like to obtain tickets. There was only one problem, you had to go up to London and queue for the tickets. We were all considering how we were going to do this when Dick Cody arrived home, following a trip with the US Air Force to maintain his flying capability. He said he was so tired he could sleep anywhere, so he was immediately sent up to London with a camp bed to sleep outside the theatre. At about 3.00 a.m. he was woken by a lady, 'Have you seen my pussy?' Apparently she had brought her cat up to London to queue with her. Early in the morning, Alastair Christie arrived to join the queue, so Dick drove home to commence a day's work. In the early evening my wife, Helen, and Dick's wife, Marilyn, arrived to join the queue so that Alastair could go home. Apparently the American press had heard about these strange British that sleep in the roads of London to obtain ballet tickets, and they were most surprised to interview the wife of an American officer who had joined them. Early on the Tuesday morning they were given tickets which indicated their queue position and they returned at 10.00 a.m. to buy the theatre tickets. These days people seem to sleep in the roads only when they are drunk! We all had the pleasure of enjoying the dancing of Margot Fonteyn and Rudolf Nureyev.

In June 1966 I was posted to the Ministry of Aviation, which seemed a very odd appointment. When I arrived at my new post I was informed that the Ministry was concerned with some of the modifications to RAF aircraft and had decided that an RAF pilot should be appointed with the responsibility to agree all modifications. Apparently an aircraft had been modified and the control was in a position that the pilot could not reach, thus it was decided that a pilot would sign the 'approval' for all aircraft modifications. I recall that my first lunch was with the chief test pilot at Handley Page, who manufactured the Victor, so presumably I was seen as an important person.

I visited Boscombe Down and flew the Heron, Meteor 7, and Shackleton. A couple of months after I was appointed, there was an important meeting at which all the staff were to attend, apart from me. I went to see my commanding officer and asked why was I the only member of the staff who was not attending the briefing? He sat quietly for a couple of minutes and said:

By the end of the week I expect to be informed that you are being posted to command a Vulcan squadron. I believe that you will shortly be sent on a refresher flying course, then off to RAF Finningley to fly the Vulcan. I cannot imagine a more satisfying and challenging posting and I wish you the very best of luck.

HANDLEY PAGE VICTOR

The Handley Page Victor was the final V-bomber to become operational in the RAF and the last to be fully retired. For the majority of its service it was used in an aerial refuelling role, although it was designed and commissioned as part of the UK's nuclear deterrent programme and served for ten years in that capacity.

Along with Avro, Armstrong Vickers, and several smaller aviation firms, Handley Page received Specification B.35/46 from the Ministry of Supply, which asked for a medium-range bomber capable of carrying a 10,000-lb bomb, reaching an altitude of 50,000 feet, and cruising at up to 575 mph. Speed and height rather than cannons were to act as the aircraft's defences.

Handley Page proposed a crescent-shaped wing design to give the aircraft, designated HP.80, the required cruising speed. Initially, a tailless version was considered, but this was scrapped in favour of a high-mounted tailplane. After careful alterations in the size and angle of the crescent wing to reduce buffeting, Handley Page submitted their design to the Air Ministry and received an order to construct a prototype.

On 24 December 1952, WB771, the first of two prototypes built concurrently took to the air. Both prototypes were performing well until, on 14 July 1954, the second aircraft, WB771, crashed when its tail ripped off during a low-level pass at RAF Cranfield, killing all four members of the crew. The stress and fatigue on the tailplane had been underestimated; to remedy the fault an additional bolt was added and ballast weights were loaded into the nose to distribute stress on the airframe. The overall design was modified by lengthening the nose (which also provided a safer escape route for the crew in an emergency) and shortening the fin on the tailplane.

By this stage the HP.80 had been officially named the Victor B.1 and twenty-five had been ordered by the Air Ministry; in May 1955 a further thirty-three were added to that number. Production Victor B.1s were powered by Armstrong Siddely Sapphire ASSa.7 turbojet engines and initially equipped with the Blue Danube nuclear weapon. Between 1958 and 1960, twenty-four B.1s were given a larger tailcone to house radar

Crew of a
Victor Mk2
running to
their aircraft.

A Victor
Mk2 being
serviced.

Rear view
of a Victor
Mk2 being
serviced.

Rear view
of a Victor
Mk2.

warning receivers and electronic countermeasures, and were given the designation B.1A.

In April 1958, No. 10 Squadron of RAF Cottesmore became the first squadron to be equipped with the Victor B.1, followed shortly by No. 15 Squadron. Meanwhile, four B.1s joined the Radar Reconnaissance Flight at RAF Wyton. Because of the enormous responsibility shouldered by V-Force crews and the fact that, on a nuclear strike, each Victor would have operated entirely independently, special attention was given to crew training and assimilation. Personnel operating the Victor could expect to remain in the same crew for up to five years to ensure absolute confidence in one another. Flight training, however, was limited to a single five-hour training sortie per week to preserve the fatigue life of the aircraft.

The V-Force was intended to be a rapid response force: when on Quick Reaction Alert (QRA), Victor crews were trained to have their aircraft airborne within four minutes. Navigators were trained to follow

The tail of a Victor Mk2.

carefully planned flight routes to avoid Soviet defences while using electronic countermeasures to remain undetected. With the introduction of surface-to-air missiles in the Soviet arsenal—as demonstrated by the shooting down of Gary Powers' U-2 spy plane over Russia in 1960—the Air Ministry changed its tactics to strike at low-level. This was done alongside the development of 'standoff' nuclear missiles, particularly the Avro Blue Steel and the abortive US Skybolt missile.

Despite the change to low-level tactics, the Victor B.2 had been designed to reach a higher service ceiling. The original B.1 design was given more powerful Rolls-Royce Conway engines and modified dramatically with an extended wingspan, a new electrical system, and redesigned wing roots, intakes, and engine boxes. The first Victor B.2 entered service in the RAF in February 1962, and shortly afterwards this specialist high-altitude flyer was given a low-level role, marked by its new camouflaged colour scheme. In 1964, the B.2 also began carrying the Blue Steel missile, although the more advanced US Skybolt missile

A Blue Steel missile on a lorry with a Victor Mk2 in the background.

was eagerly anticipated; a single Victor would be able to carry four Skybolts (two under each wing) and only one Blue Steel missile. As a result, the Air Ministry cancelled several Victors already in production, unaware that the Skybolt itself was to be cancelled mid-development. The order for the Victors was later reinstated, but Handley Page was under increasing pressure from the British Government to merge with one of its competitors, making the future of the company uncertain.

With the withdrawal of the Valiant fleet due to fatigue in 1964, the Victor B.1A was hurriedly converted to an aerial tanker role, receiving a two-point system with a hose and drogue carried under each wing. This was later upgraded to a three-point system. The following year Victor B.1As were deployed to RAF Tengah, Singapore, to serve as a deterrent to Indonesia during the Borneo conflict. Although converted to tankers, the B.1As retained their conventional bombing capacity. In the event, the Victors were never called upon to carry out a bombing sortie.

After the passing of the role of nuclear deterrent to the Royal Navy's submarine-launched Polaris missiles in 1969, the Victor's primary role was as an aerial refuelling tanker, for which there was a great demand in the RAF, although some Victors were also used for strategic reconnaissance in the Mediterranean and South Atlantic. In its tanker role, the Victor served in the 1982 Falklands War, refuelling its fellow V-bomber, the Vulcan, in the famous Blackbuck Raids. They were the longest bombing raids ever attempted at the time, with each sortie requiring more than a million gallons of fuel and eleven Victors to support a single Vulcan. The Victor's final operational sorties came in 1991, when eight Victor K.2s (a later tanker variant) were deployed to Bahrain to support coalition aircraft in an aerial refuelling capacity during the Gulf War. The Victor crews distinguished themselves with a 100-per-cent success rate in 299 sorties.

By 1993, the Victor fleet had been retired from service in the RAF. Shortly after this conflict, the remaining Victor fleet was retired. Most Victors were scrapped or used as fire training aids, but five examples still survive.

10

Commanding No. 27 Squadron
Flying the Vulcan Mk 2

In November 1966, I was posted to RAF Manby on a refresher flying course to fly the Jet Provost. When I review my flying it highlights the difference between a General List Officer and other aircrew. I arrived at the RAF College at Cranwell in September 1950, commenced flying in May 1951, and was commissioned in April 1953. In May 1953 I was trained to fly jet aircraft, specifically the Meteor, and in retrospect came very close to ending my life. In November I was trained to fly the Canberra and at that time there were no dual-control aircraft, so it was another interesting challenge. In February 1954 I was posted to No. 90 Squadron based at RAF Marham, in Norfolk. The squadron had been flying the Washington or in US terminology, the B-29, and I was the first Canberra pilot to join the squadron. I had a fascinating eighteen months flying all around the Middle East in a completely different world from that of the twenty-first century. In October 1955 I was posted on No. 1 Second Pilots' Course to fly the Valiant, the first V-bomber to enter RAF service, and in November I joined No. 138 Squadron, the first Valiant squadron in the RAF. In October and November 1956 I bombed Egypt in the Suez War. In March 1957 I was sent on a Valiant captain's course and in June joined No. 90 Squadron at RAF Honington and remained until May 1961. In June I was promoted to Squadron Leader and in August joined No. 7 Squadron at RAF Wittering as a flight commander. With the introduction of the Vulcan Mk 2 and the Victor Mk 2, the Valiant was the 'old' aircraft of the deterrent force thus it was decided to disband No. 7 Squadron; in October 1962 I flew the last Valiant from RAF Wittering. With the operational change to potentially low-level penetration of Russia, the Valiant developed structural fatigue problems and was grounded in December 1964. However, my flying life changed with the disbandment of No. 7 Squadron and in 1963 I spent a year at the RAF Staff College, followed by service at Bomber Command Headquarters in Buckinghamshire until June 1966, then four months at the Ministry of Aviation and back to flying following about four years 'on the ground'.

The Jet Provost was a delightful aircraft to fly and I was sent solo after just three hours' flying. In retrospect I find it interesting that after four years

PJG having just arrived at Tucson AFB Arizona with 27 Squadron in March 1968.

An airborne Vulcan Mk2 in camouflage design for low-altitude flying.

working in staff appointments, I was sent solo after just three hours of flying. I completed forty-five hours flying by day and night, including enjoyable hours flying at low level, which presumably was to prepare me for flying the Vulcan.

In January 1967 I was posted to No. 230 Operational Conversion Unit at RAF Finningley, just south of Doncaster, to be trained to fly the Vulcan Mk 2. I spent thirty-three hours in a flight simulator to complete ten training exercises before I got anywhere near the Vulcan. I recall that I found the simulator exercises most difficult but fortunately passed the 'tests' so in March commenced flying the Vulcan. Following five dual trips, was sent solo and then completed a total of fifty-eight hours to pass my final handling. Interestingly my final handling trip was in Vulcan 558 which was the aircraft used to bomb the Falkland Islands and in 2014 is the one Vulcan still flying. After four years 'on the ground', I was back to command a Vulcan squadron after just over 100 hours of flying.

In May I was posted to RAF Scampton just north of Lincoln to command No. 27 Squadron. The squadron had eight Vulcans Mk 2 and eleven crews. During my years flying the Valiant, I was flying a white aircraft with the plan to attack Russia at high level and drop a nuclear weapon. All the aircraft at

A Blue Steel missile being fitted to a 27 Squadron Vulcan Mk2 at RAF Scampton

Scampton in Nos 27, 83, and 617 Squadrons were camouflaged and fitted with a Blue Steel missile, which meant we would approach Russia at high level and then descend to low level to launch a missile about 50 miles from our target. We did not have the fuel to return to base so presumably would have turned port (left) with the hope of reaching Sweden or possibly another neutral country. In 1967 the three squadrons at Scampton all had an aircraft on alert and fitted with a Blue Steel missile. The aircraft had been modified so that the four engines could effectively be started simultaneously and it could be airborne in less than four minutes.

Life on a military base depends upon the operational requirements. During the Cold War, RAF crews and support staff of operational units were required to live on base, so when I was posted to Scampton, my wife and I had to live in the married quarter, despite having bought our home in Buckinghamshire. The administrative staff led a normal working life of working from 8.30 to 5.00 p.m. with a break for lunch. The technical staff had engineers on alert to prepare aircraft for take-off within minutes. For the aircrew it meant being on alert for about one day every week, with breaks for trips overseas and holidays. A day on alert would consist of arriving at the Operations Office at

The Blue Steel Missile.

Loading Blue Steel onto a Vulcan Mk2.

A camouflaged Vulcan Mk2 with Blue Steel.

about 8.oo a.m., checking the weather and the route, and then commencing the twenty-four-hour 'alert' duty at 9.oo a.m. with a check of the aircraft. We had five-berth caravans where the crew had their own cabin, slept in their flying kit and could be in the operational aircraft within minutes. The varied working hours with day and night flying, overseas trips and alert duty, meant that all aircrew led very different lives. I recall one day phoning my station commander, Group Captain Alan Mawer, and requesting a meeting. I arrived at his office and he said 'You have come to ask my advice about what action we should take regarding Flight Lieutenant YYYY who is having an affair with Squadron Leader XXXX's wife. Am I right?' In a small community it is difficult to keep some secrets!

Our routine flying was vastly different with low-level flying on most sorties. We would fly up to Scotland and fly around in areas where we would not cause noise problems. In October my crew flew out to Goose Bay in Labrador and flew three low-level sorties over Northern Canada, where the terrain is similar to that of Russia and the only inhabitants we could upset were the bears. The winter temperatures in Labrador are very low and if an aircraft was planned to fly, the ground crew would move the aircraft into the hanger, refuel it, and tow it back to the parking area. The crew would check the

A Vulcan B2 being refuelled.

refuelled and 'warm' aircraft and take-off for a low-level sortie over Northern Canada—a challenging flight. One day the ground crew were repeating a routine movement of a Vulcan into the hanger; they refuelled the aircraft and were towing it back when it suddenly dropped through the floor. Apparently there were hot air ducts underneath the hangar. Fortunately none of the ground crew were injured, but if someone had been in the wrong location they could have been killed. The Vulcan suffered serious damage so an enquiry was needed. I was appointed the President of the Board of Enquiry and flew out to Goose Bay with two engineering officers. The engineers assessed the damage to the aircraft and noted the replacement equipment that was required, and also explained why the accident had occurred. We had interesting interviews with many ground crew and they all seemed to think that they would be held responsible. The very serious members of the Board of Enquiry asked all the right questions and when the interviewees left, we burst into laughter as we knew those who were very seriously worried had absolutely no responsibility for the accident. As the hanger was owned and managed by the Canadian Air Force we endeavoured to speak to a representative of the RCAF, but the response was total silence. Eventually I sent a signal to the Ministry of Defence saying that we could not complete our task as we required a structural engineer who could examine and assess the structure of the hanger. A qualified engineer was immediately flown out to Goose Bay and he examined the hanger, the damage to the floor, and the damage to the Vulcan. He produced his report and stated that no aircraft heavier than an Anson should ever be permitted to go into the hanger—an Anson was about one twentieth of the weight of a refuelled Vulcan. Having completed our task, we returned to the

UK; I have absolutely no idea of the discussions between the RAF and the RCAF. Since the RAF wished to use the facilities at Goose Bay, I presume there was a friendly agreement and the RAF paid for the repair to the Vulcan.

In March 1968 I was appointed the detachment commander when two Vulcans were required to participate in the Aerospace and Arizona Celebrations at Davis-Monthan Air Force Base in Tucson, Arizona. My crew were accompanied by a Vulcan from No. 617 Squadron and we flew to Goose Bay in Labrador, Offutt AFB in Nebraska, and on to Davis-Monthan. I recall that Air Traffic asked me to fly 5 miles to starboard of our track so that passengers in civil airliners could see this strange aircraft.

Davis-Monthan is a unique airfield. Arizona is a very dry and warm, and 3,000 acres of dry desert is used to store US aircraft. In 1968 there were about 4,000 aircraft from the Army, Navy, and Air Force all stored in the desert—the only time I have ever seen such a collection of aircraft. Unfortunately the RAF has never had such a facility, so wonderful aircraft like the Valiant were destroyed.

The visit to Tucson was a memorable event with many thousands coming to see the display. It being a desert, people come in light clothes, but on the Saturday afternoon there was a light shower so many went under the wings of the Vulcan to keep dry. I took a photo and sent it back to the RAF with the heading 'Americans sheltering under Britain's Nuclear Deterrent'. The photo was published with a slightly altered heading.

PJG (right) having arrived at Davis Monthan Air Force Base in Nevada for air show, March 1968.

This page: A Vulcan at Davis Monthan Air Force Base in Nevada.

An RAF Vulcan at Davis Monthan Air Force Base, Nevada.

A 617 Squadron Vulcan arriving at Davis Monthan Air Base, Nevada.

In January 1968 Group Captain D. J. Furner was appointed station commander of RAF Scampton, the first navigator to command a V-Force Station. As a general duties officer, he regarded the appointment as normal. The MoD decided that many of the original historical commands in the RAF should be 'retired'. In April, Bomber Command was to become part of history; the stand down parade would be held at Scampton on 29 April. I was responsible for hosting all the very important visitors, and top of the list was Marshal of the RAF Sir Arthur Harris. There were many guests including the Rt Hon. Denis Healey, Secretary of State for Defence, Marshal of the RAF Lord Portal, Marshal of the RAF Sir Charles Elworthy, Sir Barnes Wallis, and three Bomber Command holders of the Victoria Cross, namely Group Captain G. L. Cheshire, Wing Commander R. A. B. Learoyd, and Warrant Officer N. Jackson. The parade and march past were executed to perfection and the Bomber Command Pennant was ceremoniously lowered for the last time as an Avro Lancaster dipped in salute overhead. The Strike Command Pennant was raised and No. 617 Squadron executed a scramble with three Vulcans.

All the VIPs went to the Officers' Mess where there was a formal lunch for the important guests and a casual meal for the majority. I remember meeting Sir Barnes Wallis, the man behind the momentous Dam Busters raid—probably the most famous aircraft operation in history. Shortly after the formal lunch had commenced a tannoy message told me to report to the C-in-C immediately. 'Where is Sir Arthur Harris?' he said. 'Sir, he is in the lounge surrounded by every young officer on the station and I doubt if he will come in for the lunch.'

In my opinion, Sir Arthur Harris, as the C-in-C of Bomber Command, had the most difficult task of any RAF commander. If he sent aircraft to Target 'A' they might lose ten aircraft, but if sent them to Target 'B' they might lose a hundred aircraft. The strain of making such decisions for three years is beyond belief.

A few years ago there was a letter in the *Daily Telegraph* from the Russian interpreter at the Yalta Conference, stating that Stalin demanded that the RAF and the USAF should stop the German reinforcement of the Eastern front. If you look at a map of Germany there is one major target for reinforcement to the east, Dresden. War is an undesirable activity but defeating the enemy has top priority, even if it means that wonderful cities are destroyed. My personal respect for Sir Arthur Harris has no limitation. I believe that the young officers at Scampton demonstrated their respect for the person responsible for the most challenging task of any RAF officer. He attempted to get a special medal for Bomber Command but this was refused. However, it is well known that 55,573 aircrew of Bomber Command lost their lives and the country has now shown its respect with the building of the Bomber Command Memorial at Green Park in London.

PJG with MRAF Sir Charles Elworthy, the Chief of the Air Staff, at the Stand Down of Bomber Command at RAF Scampton on 29 April 1968.

PJG with Marshals of the RAF Sir Charles Elworthy and Sir Arthur Harris, with Wing Commander A. Christie, also CO of a Vulcan squadron. Stand Down of Bomber Command on 29 April 1968.

The actions of Bomber Command are still frequently discussed, mainly by those who hold strong views and yet have little understanding of military operations. On 14 February 2014 there was a letter in *The Times* from a Church of England bishop, and I quote part of his letter:

> [...] next year's 70th anniversary of the Dresden bombing will mark an appropriate occasion for our Government to acknowledge the suffering of the city then and to express sympathy with those that still bear the scars.

Britain and the United States entered the war as a result of the actions of Germany and Japan. At the Yalta Conference, held from 3 to 11 February 1945, Stalin demanded that the RAF and the USAF should bomb Germany to stop the reinforcement of the eastern front and thereby bring an end to the war. An examination of a map of Germany explains why Dresden was attacked on 13 and 14 February—it was to destroy the rail communications to the east, but it inevitably resulted in the destruction of an historical city. Three months later, the war in Europe ended on 8 May 1945. Historical records show that when ordered to bomb Dresden, Sir Arthur Harris required a written instruction. It is a sad fact of war that historical cities like Coventry and Dresden have been badly damaged, but it is factually and ethically wrong to blame those who planned and participated in the attacks. It is the responsibility of the military to win a war as quickly and efficiently as possible. I have read an interesting comment by Field Marshal Montgomery regarding Sir Arthur Harris:

> I doubt any single man did more in winning the war than he did and I doubt whether that is generally realised.

Returning to the stand down parade, at which Sir Arthur Harris was our most honoured guest, I still have a letter from Group Captain Furner dated 30 April 1968:

> I write to express my sincere appreciation of the efforts you made to ensure the success of the hosting plan on April 29th. With a guest list such as we had, a poorly contrived hosting plan could have soured the day. Yours went splendidly. Well done, Host One!

While at Scampton I had two other unusual jobs. The first was to escort the commander-in-chief of a visiting air force. The Dutch C-in-C arrived at Heathrow and I met him with his attaché and took him to his hotel in London. I was staying in the RAF Club and phoned the personal staff officer responsible for the visit to tell him that I would like a better staff car, whereupon I was informed that there was nothing wrong with the car. On the Tuesday morning

Marshals of the RAF, Sir Charles Elworthy, Lord Portal, and Sir Arthur Harris, with Wing Commander A. Christie, at the Stand Down of Bomber Command on 29 April 1968.

I collected the C-in-C from the hotel and delivered him to the MoD, where he met the Air Force Board and had lunch. After lunch, he came out to the car and got in, with the Air Force Board all saluting his departure. But the driver could not start the car. A group of drivers pushed the car down the road and fortunately the engine started. By the time I had returned to the RAF Club and was informed that I would have a different staff car.

My second unusual duty was again to escort a C-in-C, this time General Errazuriz Ward, the C-in-C of the Chilean Air Force. He visited in March 1969 and was staying at the Savoy Hotel. On the Monday he spent the day at the MoD and met all the appropriate high ranking staff, including the head of defence sales. On the Tuesday he drove to Northolt and the Queen's Flight flew him and his entourage to RAF Upavon and then to RAF Abingdon. He departed from Abingdon in a Queen's Flight helicopter, which took him to Headquarters Strike Command. On Wednesday he departed Strike Command in a helicopter to Benson and transferred to an Andover of the Queen's Flight to RAF Waddington, from where he returned to Northolt and then back to the Savoy Hotel and dinner at the Chilean Embassy. On Thursday it was by car to Northolt and then aboard a Queen's Flight Andover to Little Rissington, the base of the Central Flying School, with a presentation and flight in a Jet Provost. After a return to Northolt it was back by car to the Savoy Hotel for formal entertainment in the evening, bringing the official visit to an end. The

RAF and those responsible for defence sales provided a most superb visit. I wonder if such visits are organised in the twenty-first century.

In an RAF station with three aircraft permanently armed with nuclear weapons, there was always a duty officer available. One Saturday, I was the duty officer and was asked to go to Air Traffic Control immediately. The captain of an RAF freighter was returning from Germany with a cargo of nuclear warheads for servicing in the UK. He above RAF Scampton but could not get his undercarriage down—we agreed that the matter should not be discussed with other agencies as the whole of the UK could suddenly be made aware of the dangers of a major nuclear accident. He said that the undercarriage was partly down but he could not get the green lights to show that it was locked down. Apparently the undercarriage worked on a screw system rather than the usual hydraulic system, so that if the undercarriage was partially down it should not retract. We agreed that he should do a normal approach but overshoot so that we could visually check the undercarriage. He did a controlled approach and the undercarriage touched the runway, followed by an overshoot. The green lights came on, so the undercarriage *was* locked down. He did a normal landing and was met by about twenty RAF fire engines. The thought of an aircraft with nuclear warheads making a landing with a faulty undercarriage ... but thankfully the problem was solved.

One of the pleasant activities at most RAF stations is to hold a reception for the local important people, such as MPs, mayors, councillors, farmers, and those that live on the approach to the airfield. The parties are normally organized for September or October and are friendly and relaxed events. On one occasion the party had gone on for about an hour when suddenly all the lights went out. Before the problem could be investigated, the lights came back—but then it emerged that the Mayor of Gainsborough had lost his chain of office. He was a supporter of CND, the Campaign for Nuclear Disarmament, and this clearly had something to do with the theft. I believe a group of young officers decided that they would demonstrate their disapproval of the mayor. They checked the control of the lights in the Officers' Mess, had a close examination of the chain of office and planned the operation to perfection. The message from above was that if the chain of office was returned undamaged by midday on Monday, no action would be taken. It was returned undamaged.

No. 27 Squadron had not held a reunion so it was agreed that we would arrange a gathering in November 1968. The squadron was originally formed in 1916 and flew the Martinsyde G 100 Scout which became known as the 'Elephant'. The derivation is obscure and was probably due to the size of the aircraft, but the squadron badge featured an elephant so obviously an elephant should feature in our reunion. We negotiated with Hucknall Zoo and arranged to adopt an eight-month-old Indian elephant which we christened as 'Flying Officer Gosta'; at 11.00 a.m. on 8 November she inspected the

27 Squadron Reunion held at RAF Scampton in November 1968, with PJG having a chat with Gosta, 90 Squadron's adopted elephant.

squadron. There were hundreds of spectators, including the national press, and this small elephant behaved immaculately. During the evening we held an anniversary dinner again attended by Gosta and many former members of the squadron. We asked Sir Hugh Chance if he would speak as he served on the squadron in 1916. It was a fascinating talk about life in the air during the First World War; I recall that he was sent to France with only something like twenty-five flying hours. The final event was a talk by a director of Hawker Siddeley who presented the squadron with a silver model of the Vulcan. It was a memorable day for all those that attended.

May Day is always an interesting time of the year, when people undertake various activities often to raise money for charities. However, nuclear disarmament campaigners used the occasion to visit RAF stations and USAF units. As aircraft fitted with nuclear weapons were well guarded, the CND would remain outside the grounds. One night I was escorted by a couple of military police as we walked around the base to ensure that no one had managed to make it on to base and we came across an RAF member enjoying sex with a

PJG in the Officers' Mess at RAF Scampton with the elephant Gosta wanting a drink!
27 Squadron Reunion in 1968.

Sir Hugh Chance speaking at the 27 Squadron Reunion. Sir Hugh served on the squadron in 1916.

PJG with Gosta the elephant at the 27 Squadron Reunion.

The squadron aircrew cheering Gosta.

27 Squadron march past with Gosta.

young CND supporter. It had never occurred to me that the secondary task of the CND was to ensure that military personnel were well entertained.

My two years as the commanding officer of No. 27 Squadron included low flying over Canada, the UK, Denmark, and Libya, and air displays in the USA and the UK, but No. 27 Squadron was primarily part of the UK nuclear deterrent. As I have already said, all crews spent about one day a week on alert, apart from leave and overseas trips. I am frequently asked if the crews accepted this responsibility happily. I believe that aircrews acknowledged that we were a deterrent and therefore did not spend their time thinking about dropping a nuclear weapon. A while ago I met someone who said that a friend of his had been a Vulcan captain and had decided that he could not accept the responsibility of dropping a nuclear weapon. He visited a Church of England minister serving in the RAF and was 'retired' from the RAF in days. I have no personal record of such actions and presumably such decisions would be regarded as confidential or secret.

Two ground crew in front of a 27 Squadron Vulcan.

With nuclear weapons involved, there was an obvious need for security to ensure that top secret information was not passed to a potential enemy. Homosexuality was illegal at the time and could therefore be used as a tool for blackmail to obtain information. We were positively vetted regarding our political views, drinking habits, financial position and sexuality. We were asked to assess others and give the names of those who could assess us. I recall being interviewed by a team of three senior officers who were apparently responsible for monitoring security within the V-Force, but I was not informed of any serious issues.

In the years that the RAF provided the nuclear deterrent, there were constant changes in the equipment provided and the proposed means of attack on Russia. When I was flying the Valiant I was flying a white painted aircraft with the intention of a high-level penetration, but when I commanded No. 27 Squadron we were flying a camouflaged aircraft with the intention of entering enemy territory at low level. With the development of the Blue Steel, trials were initiated in which the missile was launched 47 miles from the target and had an impact error of 1,065 yards. Another was launched 35 miles from the target with an impact error of 515 yards. The plans were that we should approach the target at high level and then descend at anything from 350 to 550 miles from the target and approach at low level. Depending on the weather, we should fly as low as 50 feet or up to 1,000 feet in poor visibility or in regions with power lines. My crew's target was the Pulkovo Airport at Leningrad, or St Petersburg as it was originally known and has now been re-named. We would climb to high level over the North Sea and then descend over the Baltic Sea, keeping as far to the north as possible and approaching Leningrad over the sea with the aim of launching our Blue Steel about 50 miles from the city. We would not have the fuel to return to the UK so would turn port and fly up to Finland or Sweden, presumably with the intention of baling out and wondering about our future. Fortunately it was a mission that we never undertook.

While I was serving at Scampton we had three squadrons with eight Vulcans on each, and all were equipped with the Blue Steel. Every crew spent a proportion of their time on alert, and had no knowledge of the targets of other crews. The Operations Wing on the station controlled air traffic and held all the target information, which was obviously top secret. It was presumed that no aircraft would have the fuel to return to the UK, so that those attacking targets in the north would turn port and hope to reach a neutral country, whereas those attacking targets to the south would turn starboard and head towards a country believed to be neutral. The plans were all made but fortunately never executed.

A few years after my retirement from the RAF, I flew to Moscow and enjoyed exploring the city, but I had the feeling that I was being watched.

Blue Steel being downloaded from a truck.

Ground crew preparing the Blue Steel missile to be fitted to a Vulcan.

Ground crew preparing to load a Blue Steel missile to a Vulcan Mk2.

A Vulcan Mk2 and the Blue Steel missile.

A Blue Steel missile fitted to a Vulcan Mk2.

We went to the Russian ballet and noticed security people who appeared to be paying special attention to us. There was certainly a security team in our hotel, but maybe that was normal in those far off days. My wife and I then went by train to St Petersburg and the Pulkovo Airport was increasing in size. Anyone who has visited St Petersburg will know that it is one of the most interesting cities in the world, and thankfully still standing.

When flying an aircraft such as the Vulcan, it is essential that all pilots are regularly checked both during the day and night. For example in October 1968, I am recorded as giving a night check to four pilots, and if I had not flown by night, then I required the same check. We also had regular simulator checks which ensured that we were aware of our emergency procedures. If a pilot was failing to present the appropriate professional standards, he could be returned to the Operational Conversion Unit for a refresher course. One of our co-pilots failed to maintain the required professional standards so I wrote to the personnel management staff requesting that he be withdrawn from No. 27 Squadron and retrained on a less demanding aircraft. The personnel staff at the MoD decided that he should be retired from the RAF entirely and for some inexplicable reason sent a copy of my letter to his father. Apparently the RAF were then threatened with legal action as I had recommended that 'he should be retrained on a less demanding aircraft'. Unfortunately this disagreement continued for weeks, which was an irritating distraction from the responsibility of managing No. 27 Squadron. I recall that many years later we met at the RAF Club in London when the man in question was a civil airways captain.

A critical part of maintaining a V-Force base in the RAF was ensuring that the wives and children of RAF personnel were able to live full and happy lives without the concerns of nuclear operations. There was a school on the Scampton base for the young children, and the wives participated in many activities. I have a copy of the RAF Scampton magazine *Delta*, which says the following about the play, *A Breath of Spring*:

> It was Helen Goodall and Polly Headlam who made the best of their parts. Helen Goodall brought to the role of Dame Beatrice a vitality and charm which made 'Bee' a most enduring lady, the only problem being that Mrs Goodall is manifestly not around the fifty mark.

This was just one of the numerous social events to create an enjoyable atmosphere on base. I also have a photo of a No. 27 Squadron party showing the wives of the squadron aircrew all dressed to demonstrate their affection for the elephant!

In May 1969 I was sent on a Western Ranger via Goose Bay to Offutt where I was to give an air display in the Vulcan at the Armed Forces Display. A month later I was destined to hand over command of No. 27 Squadron and leave Scampton.

I believe that Scampton was a professionally managed station that had the capability to launch a nuclear-equipped force. Throughout the Cold War the V-Force was modified and improved at a modest cost. The role was changed from high level to low level but it retained its capability.

In June 1969 I handed over command of No. 27 Squadron and was sent to the RAF College of Air Warfare at Manby in Lincolnshire, where I would spend six months. No. 18 Course comprised one Group Captain, twelve Wing Commanders and two United States Lieutenant Colonels—one Air Force and one Navy—all of whom were either pilots or navigators. The aim was that we would examine the structure, responsibilities, and future of the RAF and the United States air power. We visited RAF stations operating all types of aircraft and had the pleasure of flying a Lightning Mk 4 and intercepting a Vulcan,

27 Squadron party at RAF Scampton in 1968 with the ladies in 'elephant' attire. The CO of Scampton, Group Captain Mawer, is one of the guests.

27 Squadron wives at a Christmas party, all dressed in their 'elephant attire', with one questionable female?

and we even returned to Scampton to fly the Vulcan. We also visited Northern Ireland to examine the political and religious problems in the company of armed police, and went to Europe to spend time at the Supreme Headquarters Allied Powers. We visited RAF stations in Germany and then flew to Cyprus, Singapore, and Hong Kong, and were taken by helicopter to the Chinese border where we saw a huge portrait of Chiang Kai-shek on display in the nearest village. It was a fascinating six months spent considering the future of the RAF.

Wing Commander Jack Wilson, who commanded No. 7 Squadron when I was attached to that squadron as a Flight Commander, was also on the Air Warfare course. Jack told me that when the squadron was disbanded in October 1962, he considered that he had given excellent reports on the performance of his two flight commanders, but when he saw the reports given to those in Fighter Command, he realised that one Command was intending that its members should control the RAF. Throughout my time in the RAF, we had a confidential Form 1369 which was submitted annually on all officers, but as we never saw the form, we never knew how our superiors had assessed our performance. Years after my retirement, I believe that an RAF officer threatened legal action and the assessments were read before submission. I know that many associates were concerned about the so-called 'confidentiality' of the 1369s, as you could be considered personal competition to the superior making the report. My fellow No. 7 Squadron flight commander retired as a Squadron Leader, but within months of his retirement he was an airline captain.

In October 1969, I was told to report to the RAF Personnel Department at the MoD where I was informed that I was being seconded to the United States Air Force to serve at the Headquarters of Strategic Air Command, based at Offutt Air Force Base in the state of Nebraska. I was to be flown out to Washington to be briefed by the Air Attaché, and then fly down to Nebraska. I would be accompanied by my wife and two children. I was also advised that I needed to co-operate with the Americans; it seemed that I had upset someone, but with personal reports being confidential, it was virtually impossible to discover who it was.

I was then informed that I was required to fly to the US on 19 December and fly down to Nebraska on 23 December. I was horrified. I complained that if I was to arrive at Offutt on 23 December, my family would be a major problem for everyone. Where would we stay over Christmas? How would my children spend Christmas? To me it made much better sense to fly out in early January 1970 when we would not be a problem for anyone and all the procedures could be completed without the distraction of everyone going on Christmas holiday. However, I was told that it was essential that the officer I was replacing returned to the UK promptly—I was ordered to fly out to Washington on 19 December 1969.

AVRO BLUE STEEL

The Avro Blue Steel was an air-to-surface nuclear-armed stand-off cruise missile and a vital part of the British nuclear deterrent programme. Its development came as the result of a Ministry of Supply memorandum on 5 November 1954 which predicted that by 1960, in the event of a nuclear attack, Soviet surface-to-air missiles would be advanced enough to destroy V-bombers long before they would reach their targets. Therefore, by 1960 gravity bombs like the Blue Danube, the first nuclear weapon test-dropped by a V-bomber, would be rendered obsolete.

Although Avro had no previous experience in developing guided missiles, the firm had the confidence of the Air Ministry and was chosen to design and manufacture a rocket-powered supersonic missile with a minimum 50-mile range. Initial development began in 1955 in partnership with the computing company Elliot Bros Ltd, which would work on the guidance system, and Armstrong Siddeley, which would develop the liquid fuel engine. The design of the missile was complicated by the simultaneous development of its nuclear warhead, named Green Bamboo. Avro designers therefore had to make do with guessing the exact weight and dimensions of the missile's nuclear component. Further delays were caused by accuracy problems with the Elliot guidance system and the need to develop stainless steel fabrication techniques. In the end, Green Bamboo was superseded by Red Snow, a smaller and lighter warhead with a greater yield.

In early 1961 the first low-level test firings operated by Avro Vulcans and Handley Page Victors were held successfully at the Australian Woomera range. Blue Steel, as it had been known throughout its development, was fitted with a highly advanced inertial-navigation unit which enabled it to strike its target to within 300 feet. It was powered by a two-chamber Armstrong Siddeley Stentor Mark 101 rocket engine, burning a combination of kerosene and hydrogen peroxide, and was capable of speeds up to Mach 2.3.

In February 1963 Blue Steel finally entered service with the Vulcan B.2As of No. 617 Squadron, around three years behind schedule. No. 139 Squadron was the first Victor unit to receive the missile, in September 1963. One aircraft from each Blue Steel-equipped squadron was to be on readiness as part of Bomber Command's Quick Reaction Alert (QRA).

By the time it entered service, Blue Steel was already looking outdated. Pre-launch fuelling was very slow, taking just under half an hour, and the fuel itself was dangerous to handle; the missile was highly unreliable, with

A Victor being fitted with Blue Steel.

Ground crew preparing to load a Blue Steel missile to a Vulcan Mk2.

Above: An airborne photograph of a white Viictor Mk2 carrying a Blue Steel missile.

Left: Blue Steel missile under a Vulcan Mk2.

the RAF estimating that over half would fail to fire; and its limited range meant that the V-bombers would still be vulnerable to Soviet surface-to-air missiles. To further complicate matters, in 1963 the Air Ministry switched V-bomber tactics from high-level to low-level attacks to nullify the increasing effectiveness of Soviet guided missiles. Modifications were hastily made to the fifty-one Blue Steel missiles in service, which allowed them to be launched from below 1,000 feet.

The British Government had been hoping for an alternative. The USAF Skybolt air-launched ballistic missile had a much longer range and was superior to Blue Steel in every way. The Blue Steel Mark 2, with a ramjet engine which afforded increased range and speed, was cancelled in 1960 as the development of the Skybolt would have made it obsolete before it entered service. The British nuclear deterrent programme was becoming heavily dependent on the US missile, and a diplomatic crisis was narrowly averted when the Skybolt programme was cancelled by President Kennedy in December 1962. A laydown nuclear weapon, WE.177, was hastily produced to supplement the RAF's stock of Blue Steel missiles.

With the advent of the Royal Navy's submarine-launched Polaris missile, the Blue Steel-equipped Victor and Vulcan squadrons relinquished their QRA role, the former in December 1968, and the latter in June 1969. Blue Steel was officially retired on 31 December 1970.

Aerial view of a Vulcan Mk2, XM572, carrying a Blue Steel missile.

11

Seconded to the United States Air Force

Early on the morning of 19 December 1969 we were driven to RAF Brize Norton by my father-in-law to fly to Washington. It was an uneventful flight and we arrived at Washington about mid-day. As we were leaving the aircraft I looked at the terminal building and there was someone waving whom I immediately recognised as Colonel Dick Cody, who had been on the same RAF Staff College Course and then served at Bomber Command Headquarters at High Wycombe. After all the arrival procedures Dick told us that he had changed our arrangements and we would now joining him and his family for Christmas and would fly to Nebraska on 27 December.

Dick and his wife Marilyn had quite a large house on the outskirts of Washington and could manage the last minute addition of my family of four to their Christmas gathering of their four children and Dick's parents. It was a truly wonderful introduction into the US for my family.

Over the Christmas period there was an arrangement that allowed senior American military officers to go on a tour of the White House. Dick had arranged for Commander Goodall of the US Navy and his wife to join the tour—it was a wonderful visit to the home of the President of the United States. Sadly 27 December arrived, so we flew down to Nebraska where we were met by the officer I was replacing. Offutt Air Force base had a number of houses that were available for new arrivals, so we moved into temporary accommodation which was ideal for a family of four.

One of the essential requirements for a family arriving in the US was to have a car. The officer I was replacing took us on a tour of Offutt Air Force Base and into Omaha. We visited the main Ford dealer and saw a large estate car which had been driven for about 25,000 miles. This was an ideal car for driving a family around the United States which we bought for $2,400, including the reinstatement of the Ford warranty. This was the best value car I have ever bought. As a matter of fact, I sold it to my successor in 1972 for $1,600.

Our next problem was to find a home. Our predecessor had lived in an American equivalent of a married quarter, but we decided to move into an apartment in a new development—an ideal home with two bedrooms. The management suggested that my wife should have a briefing on the new American electrical products in the kitchen. A lady duly arrived and asked Helen for an egg. She said that she had boiled an egg before, but the 'expert' asked if she had done it correctly? She then went on to explain that you place an egg in a saucepan and then add about half an inch of water, which you boil, so that the egg is actually cooked in steam. You learn something new every day.

In early January Helen and I were invited to a formal reception at the Officers' Mess for important people in the area. I was chatting to many people and one gentleman asked me how I liked American confectionary, which I thought was awful. Then he asked me about ice cream which I said was superb. He casually asked where I lived. At about 10.00 a.m. on the Monday morning the doorbell rang and my wife answered it. There was the driver of a delivery van: 'Ma'am, I am from the Omaha Ice Cream Company and I have an order of every ice cream we manufacture. Our boss instructed me to deliver the ice cream to you.' Fortunately the management of the company that owned our property had some spare refrigerators so we enjoyed a few weeks of wonderful ice cream.

As I had been seconded to serve in the United States Air Force at the headquarters of Strategic Air Command, it is important to understand the role and responsibilities of SAC and the means by which these responsibilities were executed.

STRATEGIC AIR COMMAND

In 1946 the United States Government announced the mission of Strategic Air Command—responsibility for all land-based nuclear deterrent forces of the United States. Additionally the Command was responsible for the USAF jet tanker force which conducted refuelling operations in support of other US forces. From June 1965, SAC was also tasked with conventional operations against communist forces in South East Asia. The SAC manpower comprised about 160,000, of whom 23,000 were officers and 21,000 civilians. The missile strength was 1,054 Inter Continental Ballistic Missiles and a bomber/tanker force of approximately 70 FB-111s, 400 B-52s, and 600 KC-135s. There were also the EC-135 Airborne Command Post aircraft and a reconnaissance force of SR-71s, U2s, RC-135s, and DC-130s. In addition, SAC had a varied selection of support aircraft from C-118s and T-39s to UH-1F helicopters for missile site support.

With the unique military and political importance of the Strategic Air Command mission, it was the only Department of Defense agency designated as

Refuelling cable attached to a 'V' bomber.

a 'Specified Command'. This meant that the command was directly answerable through the Secretary of Defense to the President. Since the Commander in Chief of SAC was also the Director of the Strategic Target Planning Staff, he was responsible to the Joint Chiefs of Staff for these functions.

History records that eight Presidents of the USA have died in office, and four of that number were assassinated, so there was an obvious requirement for an effective control of the nuclear arsenal in the event of the President's death. SAC was equipped with the Boeing EC-135 Airborne Command Post aircraft which entered service in 1961. While I was serving at SAC, an EC-135 with a General on board was airborne twenty-four hours a day, so that in the event of a nuclear threat, there was always the ability to launch a nuclear retaliation. A Boeing KC-135 would fly for about fifteen hours and another aircraft would take-off. When it was in position the first aircraft would land, so there was a constant rotation of aircraft with the ability to launch a nuclear retaliation. In my view, the military capability of SAC was probably the most professionally managed in history.

When I arrived at Offutt, General Bruce K. Holloway was the commander in chief. He had a fascinating military background. When the United States entered the Second World War, he was posted to China and became commander of the Army Air Force's 23rd Fighter Group and was personally credited with shooting down thirteen Japanese planes. This was followed by posts with increasing responsibility, such as commander of the United States Air Force in Europe. On 1 August 1968 he was appointed as Commander in Chief of Strategic Air Command and director of Strategic Target Planning. It was evident that he wished to ensure that politicians, journalists, and business executives understood the role of Strategic Air Command, and briefings were held on regular occasions. It so happens that I still have copies of a number of the briefings, which were effectively 'Secret' until the presentation. I quote extracts from a talk given in December 1971:

[...] This is not December 8th, 1941. We stand in the fading days of its thirtieth anniversary, in an era when Pearl Harbor, patriotism, and praise for military and industry sometimes seem history book memories. We live in a time when the term 'war effort' could well be mistaken for the work of peace protestors, and the urgent needs of defense are sometimes achieved only through the considerable efforts of civil and defense leaders.

The present needs of the US strategic forces reflect the dramatic Soviet strategic advances over the past 10 years, compared with the slower paced improvements of our own forces. I say this not to judge the past, but to cite the reality of the present. [...] Determining strategic requirements is further complicated by negotiations for arms reductions. We all hope for a world of law, not force. That we do not yet live in such a world is daily evident, as also are the concerted efforts to reach meaningful agreement in the Strategic Arms Limitations Talks. Short of such agreements, I am unable as a commander to plan forces on intent. Military leaders must make determinations based on the reality of present forces and calculations of the projected threat. The plain facts of these determinations are that the USSR—intentions aside—potentially offers the greatest physical threat to viability that the United States of America has ever faced. In this light the 1970s will be more dangerous for America than the 1940s or the 1860s or even the 1790s. America's antagonists of former times damaged its structure but could not destroy it as a nation, even after years of war. Soviet Russia could do it before lunch today, though it would be destroyed in return. The remoteness of such a probability cannot make it a lesser consideration for those charged with national defense [...]

Strategic requirements dictate that we will continue to need the very best. The people of America do not lightly grant, nor do we likely accept, the authority to control nuclear weapons. We work for all our people to have lives of productivity and to enjoy relative comfort and security, but expect much more in return. We demand absolute conformity and hear perfection from them in certain aspects of their jobs. We accept legitimate questioning, but not disobedience. No action can be allowed which might betray our great trust. You don't buy people who live up to these specifications. They have to believe in their job and their country.

For twenty-five years our servicemen and women have provided forces for deterrence. The struggle to prevent war has not been entirely successful, but the results remain a significant achievement. Today and tomorrow we recognise some of those responsible. This recognition causes us to recall times and events and people past, and to pause in appreciation.

Franklin D. Roosevelt made a projection in one of his famous Fireside Chats which seem particularly appropriate. 'We build and defend,' he said, 'not for our generation alone. We defend the foundations laid by our fathers. We build life for generations yet unborn. We defend and build a way of life, not for America alone, but for all mankind.'

I am not aware that the RAF, the Army, or Royal Navy ever held similar briefings, which possibly explains some of the articles published in the British press and the ludicrous observations of some of our MPs or our unelected members of the House of Lords. Furthermore, when we examine the Iraq War it is evident that the professional standards within the US and the UK had totally changed. If those politicians had been in power during the Cold War, I wonder whether the world in which we are now living would exist.

At SAC Headquarters, I was working with many senior officers who had been involved in military operations and it was fascinating listening to their stories. When the United States entered the Second World War, many aircraft were flown to Europe via Canada, Iceland, and Northern Ireland. A former co-pilot in a B-17 told me that when they arrived in Northern Ireland they were told to take all their belongings out of the aircraft. The B-17 had a crew of ten so the entire crew removed all of their kit. Along came a little lady who got into the B-17 all by herself. She waved to the crew and then took off to fly to England. You can imagine the reaction of the crew that had just crossed the Atlantic. After he had completed his standard twenty-five missions—after which most USAF personnel were allowed to return to the US—my friend remained in the UK and became a Mustang test-pilot for the rest of the war. It was quite a change from being the co-pilot of a B-17.

I was also informed that in 1944 the US built three nuclear weapons storage facilities at airfields in the UK, in Mildenhall, Lakenheath, and Alconbury. No nuclear weapons were ever delivered to the UK, but provision was made should the war in Europe have continued longer than expected. I wonder who made the decision and who was aware of the storage facility.

I was appointed to serve in the pilot branch in the Directorate of Operations and Training. It was considered essential that I should have some understanding of the B-52 and KC-135, so in January 1970 I was sent to Castle Air Force Base in California where the B-52 and KC-135 crews were trained. I did a short course on the B-52, followed by an eight-hour flight as a co-pilot, which was followed by a similar course on the KC-135 and a five-hour flight as a co-pilot. In February I returned to Offutt to be trained to fly the Boeing T-39, a twin-engine executive jet which had a crew of two and carried seven passengers. At that time all pilots serving on ground appointments in the USAF had to retain their flying currency as they could be called to serve in Vietnam. This rule also applied to me, so I had to be trained to fly the T-39. I successfully passed the T-39 Ground School Examination, followed by ten training flights in February, and by 14 March I had qualified to fly as a T-39 captain. This meant that as an RAF pilot seconded to the USAF, I was trusted to fly a passenger aircraft after just six weeks of training. I suggest that this demonstrates the mutual trust and respect between the RAF and USAF.

The pilots flew alternate flights in the left- and right-hand seat. The plan was that every pilot flew one day a week and one weekend a month, which meant flying anything from twenty to forty hours a month. Each week you would be asked what trip you would like and I always selected a base I had not visited, so during my years at SAC I landed at over eighty airfields in the US, and also airfields in Canada such as Ottawa International and Goose Bay in Labrador.

I have many happy memories and during my two years of flying the T-39, I never had an unfortunate incident. There was one strict rule: if there is unexpected rough weather, such as a tornado, divert and land at the nearest airfield. Apparently there had been an unfortunate incident where a crew had attempted to fly through very rough weather, so the rules were changed to avoid rough weather at all costs and land.

On one trip we were instructed to divert and land at a major SAC base. We were questioned as to who we were and why we wished to land at the base. As we were flying from Offutt, the HQ of SAC, it was presumed that we were an inspection team carrying out a check on security procedures, so were informed to land, turn off the runway, and stop. We obeyed instructions and were immediately surrounded by armed guards. We were then instructed to follow a truck until we were told to stop and close down our engines. We followed instructions and were again surrounded by armed guards. It was agreed within the aircraft that I would be the first person to get out of the aircraft, dressed in my RAF flying gear. So we opened the entrance door and I stepped out to the total surprise of all the guards.

I recall another occasion when I was to fly with my immediate boss, who was an officer of the same rank. The others in the office suggested that we go for a coffee; when they had me in private they informed me that their boss was the worst pilot in SAC. He had a good brain, they said, but his lack of flying skill had meant that he was never appointed as a B-52 captain. They told me that if ever I was feeling nervous to say 'I have control' and assume command. I understood their concern; he was an awful pilot, but fortunately the weather was fine so we had no problems.

On another occasion, I was asked to fly a military veteran to various SAC bases every day for a week. He was an ex-drug user and he was touring bases to lecture personnel on the dangers of drug abuse. I went to some of the presentations and it was fascinating to listen to a capable person who had succumbed to drugs and then managed to lift himself out of that life. When you think that this was over forty years ago, his tour around SAC bases reflects the concern within the US Air Force and the positive actions that were taken.

I had the good fortune to work for a Colonel Frank Scurlock, who was a most professional and capable officer. One day he informed me that as I would only have one tour working in the USAF, I should have the opportunity to travel around their wonderful country and therefore should have a four-week holiday every summer. I had the pleasure of three such holidays when we travelled south-west, north-west, and north-east to the Great Lakes.

Back in March 1968, when I was flying the Vulcan, I was sent to Tucson in Arizona to participate in an air show. I had met Bill Pickens there and he had entertained some members of my crew. Before the US had entered the war, Bill decided to travel up to Canada to be trained as a pilot and join the RAF. We had remained friends, so on our first holiday I drove the 1,500 miles down to Tucson to stay with Bill and his charming wife. He was involved property development and some financiers from New York were visiting during my stay.

He was flying them down to Mexico in his private aircraft and I was co-opted as a pilot. When we returned to Tucson we had to present our passports, but as the US were members of NATO, I was travelling on a NATO travel order and did not have a visa. I remember the Customs officer inspecting my documents and saying, 'What is NATO?' I guess on the Mexican border NATO had no significance. Fortunately my friend Mr Pickens was a respected member of society, so I was permitted to return to the US.

One of my pleasures in the US was playing tennis and squash, and I was included in the Offutt squash team when we played Omaha. One day I had arranged a match and my opponent phoned to say he had been called away on duty, so I was knocking a ball in the squash court when some people arrived in the gallery. 'Are you waiting for your opponent?' I explained that he had been called away on duty. 'Have you ever played badminton?' As I had played badminton, I was invited to join the group. Unbeknown to me I was playing with a USAF chief warrant officer who was modestly competent! I include the photograph with the heading, 'Major General Warren D. Johnson presents Senior Badminton Doubles Championship to English Air Force Officer Wing Commander Philip Goodall and partner USAF Chief Warrant Officer Raymond Scott. This international team took the Top Flight Badminton Club Senior Championship.' We also won other awards, and badminton was another unexpected enjoyment at Offutt.

If you bought a car in the US, you had to own it for a year to avoid import duty when taking it back to the UK. We wanted a Ford Mustang, but a new model was being developed so we had to order the car unseen. Eventually a car was delivered and we went to the garage to collect a yellow Mustang. It was a beautifully designed, powerful car. I drove it to the Offutt base and was stopped by military police for speeding; I was driving at 27 mph in a 20 mph speed limit. The police had obviously never seen a British driving licence and I was told the matter would be dealt with. Eventually, as the Senior Exchange Officer on the base, I received a letter asking me to comment on the driver of the car, a Philip James. James is my middle name but the Military Police were clearly not to know that: I responded by saying that Philip James was a most reliable officer who had just purchased a new car which possibly explained his excessive speed. No further action was taken.

When I was contemplating driving the car to the east coast to have it shipped to the UK, an empty RAF freighter arrived at Offutt and offered to fly it home for me. Sometimes one is lucky! On my return to the UK, I collected a superb right-hand-drive Mustang.

During the Cold War, the RAF and the USAF used to hold bombing competitions to assess the performance of their crews. By competing in competitions in both services it was obviously possible to assess the capability of crews and to consider professional changes, if necessary. The competitions

Opposite above: 27 Squadron Vulcan XM595 taken at Tucson Air Force Base, Arizona, in March 1968.

Opposite below: Arriving at Tucson Air Force Base in Arizona in March 1968. PJG is saluting.

Above: Major General Warren D. Johnson presenting PJG and USAF Warrant Officer Raymond Scott with the Senior Doubles Award.

were normally based at McCoy AFB in Florida. Colonel Scurlock was responsible for running the competitions, so we used to fly down to ensure everything was suitably planned. The staff said they would like to show me the hotel in which I would be staying in two weeks' time. We drove to the hotel and only the foundations had been completed. I could not believe that I had been booked into a non-existent hotel. However, in two weeks, there it was. Apparently it was constructed like a Lego set. The rooms were all pre-constructed, so they were linked together and all the builder had to do was connect the water and electricity. A two-floored hotel with a wonderful swimming pool had not existed a month earlier.

I flew down to McCoy for the bombing competition and was surprised that the USAF had hired a large sedan car so that I could drive the RAF visitors around the area. I was also given an identification card which meant I could refuel the car on the USAF base at no cost. This demonstrates the close liaison between the two services.

When the retirement date for General Holloway, the C-in-C of Offutt Air Force Base, was announced, I received a phone call from his personal staff officer for a chat. General Holloway wished to visit the UK to bid farewell to his friends in the RAF, so I made all the appropriate arrangements which I believe was a memorable 'Goodbye'. I was also honoured in return by the general with the following formal certificate:

Certificate of Degree
Wing Commander P. J. Goodall, Royal Air Force

Having been thoroughly briefed, indoctrinated, rebriefed, instructed and again rebriefed on the mysteries of aerospace in general, and the Strategic Air Command in particular, and having ventured into the subterranean depth of the Free World's citadel of aerospace power, is hereby awarded the degree of
B.S.
(Bachelor of SACology)

and as such is entitled, authorised and enjoined to share her profound knowledge and enthusiasm, whenever and wherever the slightest opportunity to do so should arise.

Given under my hand this 28th day of April 1972 at Offutt AFB, Nebraska

B. K. HOLLOWAY, General, USAF
Commander in Chief

I believe that I am the only RAF officer to receive such an award. Maybe I should place the letters BS after my signature.

General Holloway was replaced by General John C. Meyer. Soon after his appointment, he was planning to visit the UK as SAC had a team participating in the RAF bombing competition. I was invited to join the team and we flew to the UK via Torrejon Air Base near Madrid, which was another base effectively controlled by SAC. On our return trip, as we were flying over New York, I was asked if I would like to phone my wife, so I gave my phone number and had a fascinating discussion. 'You are flying over New York and talking to me? You will be home in about three hours?' It was the only time in my life that I have made a personal phone call from an aircraft.

On my return, I had my posting instructions and discovered I would be returning to Strike Command Headquarters with responsibility for nuclear planning. This totally changed my position at SAC as I was given information which was regarded as top secret. I was invited into the depths of the Headquarters and was shown the USAF and NATO nuclear war plans. When I was flying the Vulcan my target had been Leningrad, so I had a close examination to see the total number of nuclear attacks planned on that part of Russia, which I believe was something like fifteen.

The underground facilities at SAC Headquarters could be closed for twenty-eight days; they apparently had enough food and oxygen to seal the control rooms in the event of an attack for this period.

During my years at SAC, I had written articles which were published in the military press. I submitted them to the Air Attaché at the British Embassy to ensure that I was not presenting views which were contrary to British interests. As I was returning home, I asked the Editor of the SAC magazine *Combat Crew*, if I could write an amusing article. His response was that they produced professional articles not amusing ones but he could possibly make an exception. I duly submitted the following:

REMINISCENCES of an EXCHANGE OFFICER

Or: ... How I built a life-time of wonderful memories without even trying.

It was on the 6th January 1947 that the RAF and USAF agreed to exchange some seventy officers. Thus during the past twenty-five years many officers have temporarily transferred between our air forces in a wide variety of jobs ranging from flying instructors, squadron pilots or navigators, Staff College tutors to staff appointments throughout the USAF and RAF. This interchange has served to cement the close understanding and respect between our forces and in both nations has now been expanded to include other countries.

I have already recounted the stories on my first Canberra squadron and at the RAF Staff College and Bomber Command Headquarters which are examples of the close working relationship between the RAF and the USAF but my reminiscences ended, 'When my family and I return to Britain we will take with us a lifetime of wonderful memories of both the people and the countryside of North America. From my experiences and those of my associates I am convinced of the great and lasting value of the exchange scheme. Certainly I shall always cherish the unique privilege of having worked for over two years as part of the United States Air Force. When I return home I think my only problem will be my children's American accent, still I can't really blame y'all for that, as my daughter had a cultivated brogue ten minutes before we landed in Washington.

Aerial view of seven Vulcans Mk2s in formation.

1972 END OF TOUR REPORT

At the end of my exchange tour I was required to write an 'End of Tour Report'. I believe my report detailed the unique strength of Strategic Air Command which was undoubtedly the most powerful military force in history, and I believe was also the most professionally managed. My report also discussed some of the professional differences between the RAF and the USAF. When reading comments about the activities of SAC, it must be remembered that this report was written in 1972.

Intercontinental Ballistic Missiles

The total SAC ICBM strength of 1,054 missiles has remained unchanged since 1967. The fifty-four TITAN II missiles still have the capability of launching the largest weapon payloads with the tactical flexibility of storing data for three separate targets. Additionally, the re-entry vehicle has an elaborate penetration aid system which provides false targets and thus makes the real warhead. However, whilst the TITAN II force remains relatively unchanged, the total of 1,000 MINUTEMAN missiles dispersed in six wings is constantly modified. Conversion of the Minot Wing to MINUTEMAN III has been completed and it is planned that all MINUTEMAN I should be phased out by the end of 1974, leaving a force of 500 MINUTEMAN II and 500 MINUTEMAN III. The MINUTEMAN III has a new third stage with a heavier more sophisticated payload of multiple independently targetable re-entry vehicles (MIR V) and penetration aids. The MIR V payload can be controlled by its post-boost control system and each warhead and chaff decoy can be independently positioned to place them in the correct trajectory for selected targets. Additionally, the system has been updated to accommodate a wide variety of ground launch capabilities and recently an airborne launch facility has also been introduced. With a MINUTEMAN crew force of 900 officers and total maintenance authorisations for approximately 4,200 personnel, the SAC ICBM force would seem to be a most cost effective deterrent.

B-52s

One very impressive aspect of the B-52 fleet is the manner in which SAC has constantly updated the aircraft to ensure that it remains a viable weapons system. In many ways this would seem to be in sharp contrast to the RAF Vulcan force. From the recent successes of the B-52 attacks on North Vietnam it would seem that the SAC philosophy is valid. Certainly modifications to the G and H Models is continuing to ensure better penetration and survivability in the more demanding primary role. For example, one very interesting modification is the new Electro-Optical Viewing System (EVS). Apart from improving penetration capability, the EVS equipment enables the crew to make a pre-strike assessment of the target with the choice of changing the weapon aiming point. The EVS equipment includes two forward looking scanners mounted under the nose of the B-52. One of the sensors contains a low-light television camera and the second is a forward looking infra-red radar system. The visual sensors will allow the crew to see the actual terrain displayed on four TV monitors; one for each of the pilots and navigators. Other information, such as aircraft flight instrumentation and terrain avoidance radar can be superimposed as required. Another aircraft modification is the sixth modernisation of the B-52 ECM equipment in the RIVET ACE Programme. This includes consideration of such equipments as QRC-496 SMART NOISE Equipment (SNOE) for deceiving acquisition radar, ALQ-177 an active X-band jammer, modification of QRC-555-36 radar warning receiver and also new active radar tail warning device ALQ-127. Additionally, the B-52 is being modified to carry two new missiles, SRAM and SCAD, together with associated equipment which includes an inertial measurement unit and a master digital missile computer. The aircraft can carry up to 20 SRAM missiles, 8 internally and 12 externally. Initial deployment of SRAM began with the 42BW at Loring AFB It is planned that the SCAD missile should use the SRAM attachment points with the B-52 carrying up to 12; 4 internally and 8 externally. Apart from increasing effectiveness of the B-52 force by modification and re-equipment with new missiles, the alert posture of the force has also been improved. It is planned for 40 per cent of aircraft to be on alert but they are now dispersed to 9 satellite bases as well as the 22 main bases.

KC-135s

In 1972 the fleet of 600 KC-135s had one of its few modifications with the introduction of the FD-109 Flight Director System, which is a great improvement over the previous basic instrument fit. Whilst there is much discussion of a new SAC tanker, with consideration of such aircraft as the Boeing 747, DC-10 and the Lockheed Tri-Star, kit is unlikely that the KC-135s will be phased out for some years. However, an order has been placed for seven Boeing 747s to be used as Advanced Command and Control aircraft, of which the first three are destined for the US National Command Authorities.

FB-111

In 1971, FB-111 operations were concentrated into 380 BW at Plattsburgh and 509 BW at Pease. A regular training routine was established with three crews entering training every month. Both pilots and navigators complete a lead-in avionics training of 3 and 12 weeks respectively prior to the five month conversion course. The operational capability of the FB-111 has been well demonstrated by a crew with less than 30 hours winning the SAC Bombing Competition. The capability should be further enhanced when the aircraft are equipped with the SRAM missile.

Operations in South East Asia

Since June 1965, B-52s have been flying almost daily conventional bombing missions against communist forces in South Vietnam. They have also participated in interdiction operations along the Ho Chi Minh trail in Laos and more recently against military targets in North Vietnam. The D Model B-52s have been specially prepared for conventional operations and can carry a bomb load of up to 60,000 lbs with 84–500 lb or 42–750 lb carried internally and 24–500 lb or 750 lb carried externally.

The D Model aircraft have been used almost exclusively in South East Asia and have only recently been reinforced with the B-52G aircraft. Until 1970 the B-52s were flying at a rate of about 9,000 sorties a year and releasing some 250,000 tons of conventional ordnance. However, unclassified information on the more recent level of activity is not available. Apart from the B-52s, the KC-135 aircraft have also been continuously involved in large scale operations in Vietnam. Since 1965 the tankers have conducted some 650,000 refuelling operations in direct support of bomber, fighter and reconnaissance aircraft with a near 100% success rate. In fact the active participation of the SAC tanker force has made this the first conflict in which fighter-bomber and fighter-interceptor operations have not been seriously curtailed by fuel limitations.

Satellite Bases

SAC plans require 40% of bomber and tanker aircraft to be on ground alert. Dispersal of this force continues to be improved with extension of the satellite basing policy. With fewer aircraft at each base there is also an obvious reduction in launch times. Satellite crews normally remain on alert for 7 days followed by 4 ½ days for crew rest and recuperation.

Organisation of Strategic Air Command

Command and control of the SAC forces is exercised from the Headquarters at Offutt AFB through the numbered air forces or direct reporting units. 2nd Air Force at Barksdale AFB controls the major part of the bomber and tanker aircraft; 15th Air Force at March AFB is responsible for the ICBMs, the reconnaissance forces and a small proportion of the strategic aircraft; 8th Air Force at Guam commands the SAC forces in South East Asia. The 1st Strategic Aerospace Division at Vandenberg AFB has special missile responsibilities.

Public Relations and Information Service

The USAF Office of Information provides a similar service to the RAF Public Relations Department except that the USAF office is commanded and largely manned by uniformed officers and NCOs. In these days when the US military have a degree of unpopularity due to the Vietnam conflict it is most important to portray the armed services and particularly SAC in a good light. It is considered that the SAC Office of Information achieves this aim in an outstanding manner by providing a superlative service to all civilian and military agencies. These varied facilities include, the provision of excellent Information Kits which aim to sell SAC and the need for a triad of deterrent forces and not merely provide a bunch of statistics; the SAC press service which produces a weekly news sheet for the benefit of over 40 officially backed base newspapers; the Speaker service which arranges for USAF or even RAF officers to speak on a wide range of subjects from drugs to deterrents; and the execution of the Distinguished Visitor Programme which promotes regular visits to SAC Headquarters by distinguished business and civic leaders from all parts of the US who are flown to Omaha for briefings on SAC and the need for deterrent forces. These examples illustrate the aggressive positive attitude of the Office of Information which sets out to sell SAC and is not merely a cover up organisation to avoid bad publicity. In so doing the service provided is far more professional and varied than that of the sister RAF department. It is felt that this is in part due to the manning by uniformed officers and NCOs who frequently have a dedication and sense of purpose not always enjoyed by the civil servant.

EFFECTIVENESS REPORTS

The success and future of any organisation depends upon the quality of leadership. The system of assessment and selection within the organisation is naturally a matter of great interest and vital concern. The USAF and RAF have effectiveness reports which are similar in concept but different in execution. The RAF reports were confidential which meant that you did not see your assessment and were therefore unaware of any failings, unless you were informed. I am not aware that I was ever informed of any professional failing. As already mentioned, when I was on the RAF Air Warfare Course, my former No. 7 Squadron commander informed me that when he left RAF Wittering he was posted to the Personnel Department at the MoD and was horrified by the assessments of those in Fighter Command, which he interpreted as Fighter Command's aim to control the RAF. I have been informed that officers in the RAF threatened legal action if they were not shown their assessments, thus after my retirement, the policies of the RAF and USAF were effectively identical.

While serving at SAC, the colonel to whom I was responsible informed me of my assessment, and in May 1972 I was passed a copy of a letter signed by Lieutenant General Glen W. Martin, Vice Commander in Chief of Strategic Air Command, and sent to Air Chief Marshal Sir Andrew Humphrey, KCB, OBE, DFC, AFC the Air Officer Commanding in Chief of Strike Command.

Dear Air Marshal Humphrey,

Wing Commander Philip J. Goodall, our RAF exchange officer, will complete his tour with Strategic Air Command next month. Wing Commander Goodall's fine service will be reflected in his ratings as a staff officer in SAC's Operations Deputate. But I mention also his additional contributions to the SAC Command Section. Wing Commander Goodall has, throughout his tour of duty in Omaha, acted as an unofficial Ambassador to SAC from the RAF. His assistance in protocol, communication, and working level coordination has done much to enhance our association and the value of visits between our commands. General Holloway was especially appreciative of the efforts which made his last visit with you so memorable.

Sincerely …

I apologise for including this personal document, but in my opinion, I dedicated myself to ensuring a professional and close association with the US Air Force, which was, of course, a relationship of the utmost importance. I was acting as a representative of the Royal Air Force which had a reputation second to none, but will such a force exist in 2025?

The end of the Cold War was hailed as a future for democracy, but just examine the state of the world in 2015, with what seems like a permanent war in the Middle East and parts of Africa. Even commercial air liners have been shot down with the deaths of hundreds of wholly innocent people.

My 'End of Tour Report' was written in 1972 and obviously the US Air Force has changed. SAC was deactivated in 1992 and its aircraft were passed to Air Combat Command. In 2010 all the B-52 Stratofortresses relocated to the new Air Force Global Strike Command. There remain eighty-five B-52s in service, which were upgraded in 2013 and are expected to remain in service into the 2040s. I think this demonstrates the stark contrast in military planning between the US and the UK. Why did we get rid of all of our Harriers? Ask a politician, but I doubt if he or she has any understanding of defence.

TUPOLEV TU-128

The Tupolev Tu-128 (NATO reporting name 'Fiddler') was the first true long-endurance, or so-called loitering, supersonic fighter-interceptor fielded in the Soviet Union. Based on a 1950s-vintage bomber design, it boasted powerful radar and long-range air-to-air missiles, but it also came with restricted manoeuvrability. The Tu-128 was optimised from the very beginning for operating over the Soviet Union's polar territories to stop US strategic bombers approaching across the North Pole; it saw a faithful service in this difficult role in the 1960s and 1970s. It became the most notable representative of the second-generation of loitering fighters fielded by the IA PVO, tasked mainly to protect the skies of Siberia and the Far East, intercepting nuclear-armed USAF and RAF bombers *en route* to their targets that were predominantly situated in the European part of the Soviet Union.

The Tu-128 used an existing supersonic bomber design which was to be equipped with powerful radar and armed with long-range air-to-air missiles. The twin-jet fighter inherited the basic fuselage of the experimental bomber, albeit with some redesigned sections. It was mated to all-new sharply swept wings. The wing was mid-set with a slight anhedral and a swept angle of 56 degrees, using a set of low-thickness profiles. It had a straight trailing edge and was provided with a considerably increased chord on the inboard panels. The fuselage was redesigned using the area rule in order to increase the maximum speed, while the navigator's cockpit was moved behind the pilot's one; this design solution enabled the nose to be used for accommodating the bulky and heavy electronic boxes of the air-intercept radar.

The reshaped fuselage with a pronounced waist provided a better lift-to-drag ratio at subsonic cruise speeds, thus increasing the aircraft's subsonic range. The shoulder-type air intakes for the afterburning turbojets were also extensively redesigned and received moving half-cone shock bodies driven forward and aft to vary the cross section according to the flight regime. At supersonic speed the moving half-cone bodies were used to focus the shock waves on the intake lip and reduce the air intake area. Engine jet pipes were positioned side-by-side in the bulged tail.

The development of the new loitering fighter-interceptor for the PVO aviation force was formally launched by a Soviet Council of Ministers decree issued on 4 July 1958. This heavyweight intercept complex was intended to be pitted against subsonic aircraft flying at up to 21,000 m (68,880 feet) altitude.

The Tu-128 was a non-manoeuvrable aircraft which was intended to be pitted against manoeuvring targets thanks to its agile long-range missiles, capable to turn at high G when fired against manoeuvring targets. The aircraft itself was limited to turning with up to 2.4 G, while the missile was capable of reaching up to 15 G; later on the limitation was expanded to 21 G. The weapons control system enabled the Tu-128 to conduct missile engagements against targets flying 3,000 m (9,840 feet) higher than the interceptor—in this case the pilot was required to pull up at 20 degrees pitch in zoom climb towards the target just before launching its missiles.

The concept of operations of the long-range loitering interceptor called for performing the intercepts at a distance of up to 1,500 km (809 nm) from the protected objects, with up to 3.5 hours loitering time in its assigned combat patrol area. Moreover, it was not over-reliant to ground control like its short-legged predecessors equipped with small radars with limited range. The powerful radar was able to provide information for accurate missile guidance against the target during the terminal phase of the intercept.

The first Tu-28 prototype was completed in January 1961 and made its maiden flight on 18 March. During the flight testing effort, completed in mid-1964, the aircraft involved amassed a total of 799 sorties. The air intercept system designated as the Tu-128S-4 was officially commissioned in Soviet Air Defence Forces service in 12 December in 1963. The system included the R-4R (equipped with SARH seeker) and R-4I (equipped with IR seeker) air-to-air missiles, working in conjunction with the RP-S Smerch radar.

The Tu-128S-4 air intercept system was capable of performing all-aspect intercepts against targets with closure speed between 200 and 1,600 m/s (656 and 5,248 fps). The radar featured a maximum detection

Tupolev Tu-128 fighter.

range of 50 km (27 nm), while R-4 series of air-to-air missiles were made capable of hitting targets flying at between 800 and 21,000 m (2,624 and 68,800 feet) altitude and at up to 25 km (13.5 nm) range in head-on encounters. Armed with four R-4 missiles, the Tu-128 was able to fly at a maximum level speed of 1,665 kph (898 kt), while in clean configuration its maximum speed hit 1,910 kph (1.030 kt). The maximum range was 2,565 km (1,383 nm), while the practical ceiling reached 15,600 m (51,168 feet). The Tu-128 was capable of intercepting air targets at a distance of up to 1,170 km (631 nm) from the take-off airfield or the protected object, with two hours and forty minutes loitering (combat air patrol endurance) in the air.

The Tu-128S-4 air-intercept system was officially commissioned by PVO forces by a Soviet Council of Ministers decree dated 30 April 1965, with the first production aircraft taken on strength the same year. The GAZ No. 64 in Voronezh rolled out 198 Tu-128s, the last of which was handed over to the IA PVO in 1971.

12

Headquarters RAF Strike Command

Following my two and a half years at the Headquarters of Strategic Air Command, in the autumn of 1972 I was posted to the Headquarters of RAF Strike Command, formerly Bomber Command, at Naphill, close to High Wycombe in Buckinghamshire. I had responsibility for the planning of nuclear operations. My staff had an office which only three officers were permitted to enter. When they left the office it was permanently locked. Occasionally a security team would inspect the room to ensure there were no listening devices hidden in the roof or anywhere in the vicinity. Nothing was ever detected.

Soon after I arrived I discovered that the Group Captain to whom I was responsible held briefings every Friday afternoon, but I was not included them. As I had the highest security clearance of anyone at the headquarters, I was puzzled why I was excluded. One Friday I quietly walked down the corridor and listened at the door to see if I could discover the subject of the secret meetings. To my complete surprise, I discovered they were playing poker. So Friday afternoon was poker time! I have no idea of the level of their bets, but it made me wonder about the ethics of the headquarters to which I had been posted. When the Group Captain was posted, he was appointed as a station commander and I wonder about the activities on that station, which fortunately was not a V-bomber base.

When I commanded No. 27 Squadron at RAF Scampton, we were effectively the UK nuclear deterrent, but with the development of nuclear-powered submarines fitted with nuclear Polaris missiles, the V-Force was seconded to the Supreme Allied Commander Europe (SACEUR) and was fitted with a WE-177 laydown nuclear weapon. The targets were changed and tended to be further west to stop any Russian military approaches. We produced all the target information and then had the responsibility of presenting the plans at Supreme Headquarters Allied Powers in Europe (SHAPE) at Mons in Belgium. We used to fly from RAF Northolt, and because we were carrying top secret information, the aircraft would only take my staff—any others in the aircraft would present a security problem.

Every year I used to go to the BBC for a personal meeting with the technical director where I would deliver top secret instructions on radio messages to be transmitted in the event of a nuclear war. At the same time I would collect the outdated documents. These visits were always in the company of at least two officers.

One autumn it was decided that we would carry out a 'paper war' of the SACEUR War Plans to establish whether they were accurate and realistic. The 'game' played in Copenhagen. Representatives from the various NATO countries all gathered and procedures were executed successfully. On the final night, the Mayor of Copenhagen invited all participants to a reception in the Town Hall and gave a most excellent speech: 'If an organisation like NATO had been formed in the 1930s, just examine how Europe could have been saved....' I happened to be standing next to two German officers and was not sure where to look.

One day I was informed that a team of senior officers of the French Air Force were visiting Strike Command to discuss the possibility of combining our nuclear war plans. I was instructed to produce the briefings and we had a young Squadron Leader who spoke fluent French to present the RAF ideas. Unfortunately the Senior Air Staff Officer, who was a most competent and intelligent officer, went into hospital, so the deputy C-in-C was to run the meeting as the C-in-C was on a world tour before being appointed as the Chief of the Air Staff. A team of senior officers came from the Ministry of Defence. The presentations were excellent but the discussions were unbelievably awful. We bid a formal farewell to our French visitors and an Air Marshal from the MoD turned and gave the most biting criticism of an officer of air rank that I had ever heard, but his comments could not have been more accurate. I was reminded of the comments of the C-in-C of Bomber Command, who spoke at my graduation:

> In talking to you today, I want to emphasize one word. That word is 'flying' [...] in fact orders to jet squadrons written by a staff officer who is ignorant of jet flying might just as well be written in Chinese. A piston-engined pilot today is as much out of date as an archer at Agincourt [...]

As our Senior Air Staff Officer was in hospital, I recall the errors of his temporary deputy, a Group Captain in Strike Command. The top secret instructions for the control and launch of nuclear armed aircraft were distributed to all squadrons, but I pointed out that they were inaccurate, so they were immediately withdrawn. We had an exercise to bring all aircraft to alert and the First Sea Lord visited the underground control centre. The Group Captain explained how the operations were controlled but the rest of us could tell that he had a very poor understanding of what he was talking about. My staff were wondering how they could invent an explanation to support the views of the staff officer, when the Admiral thanked us for the briefing, shook my hand and winked. The Admiral obviously understood the rules for controlling the nuclear forces and realised that his escort was effectively 'an archer from Agincourt....'

Following our wonderful tour in the United States, it was nice to see old friends on our return, particularly John Cochrane and his wife. John was now the Concorde Project pilot for British Aerospace and he invited me to fly in Concorde on one of his test flights. I drove to Fairford and had the pleasure of a flight in which John was in the left-hand seat with Brian Trubshaw as his co-pilot. We flew to Mach 2 plus and completed the required tests. John and I remained good friends until his death in November 2006. He wrote superbly and a book about test flying the Concorde would have been a unique record of a brilliant pilot. He was a Scot who enjoyed life in the RAF and let us hope that his successors have the same opportunities. With his unique flying experiences, he had many stories and one particularly springs to mind while he was training British Airways pilots to fly the Concorde. He was in the cockpit monitoring his student, when an air stewardess came to him and said that there was an oil leak in the cabin. John responded by saying that there was no oil anywhere near the cabin and she must have made a mistake. She returned and assured him that there was an oil leak, so John joined her to resolve the problem. His explanation was quite simple, 'Your passenger has peed in his pants!'

One of the secondary duties that I always enjoyed was organizing the parties in the Officers' Mess, which was one of my responsibilities at Strike Command. I still have a letter I received from the wife of the C-in-C, Lady Agnes Humphrey:

> I send you my special thanks for all you did to give us such a super evening on Friday—what a monumental task you had but I hope you are feeling thoroughly renewed for your great trouble and hard work, knowing that it all went off so very successfully and well....

Nuclear weapons obviously must be maintained, so occasionally they are moved to be serviced. A great procession with vehicles escorted by the military would arouse suspicion as to the content, with obvious dangers. It was arranged that the weapons to be serviced would be driven in a minor convoy along a main road and the military would drive along a minor road in close proximity so that the nuclear weapons were effectively protected without arousing any suspicion. This was a clever plan which worked effectively during the years that the RAF provided a nuclear deterrent.

After two and a half years at Strike Command, I was due for another posting and surprisingly to the Headquarters of Allied Forces Southern Europe in Naples. This would mean my fourth tour as a Wing Commander. As

Aerial view of a Concorde in 1974.

I thought I had successful tours commanding No. 27 Squadron at Scampton and at the Headquarters of Strategic Air Command in the USA, I decided that the time had probably come for a different career and I decided to retire. I always wondered if it was the right decision, particularly as I had enjoyed my years in the RAF, but regrettably I had little respect for the manner in which Strike Command was controlled. In total contrast, I thought that Strategic Air Command in the US was probably the most efficiently operated military command in history. The Commanding General ensured that politicians, journalists, and business executives understood the role and responsibilities of SAC, thereby fulfilling their motto, 'Peace is Our Profession'.

When I retired I had the highest security classification and had a restriction on the countries I could visit for five years. I obviously respected that restriction and did not visit any countries considered a security threat.

During my years in the RAF, I enjoyed writing and, as already mentioned, when a cadet at the RAF College at Cranwell, I was awarded the Royal United Service Institute Award for my thesis, 'The History of Strategic Thought'. This was re-written in a modern format and published in 2014. I also had articles published when serving at Bomber Command and in the US at the Headquarters of Strategic Air Command. In this book about the Cold War, I have endeavoured to record the actions in which I and my close associates were involved as well as show the more human side of life in the RAF. The war in Japan ended rather more quickly than anticipated, but with the development of nuclear weapons, the political parties in the UK worked together to ensure the survival of our democracy.

Epilogue

During my years in the Royal Air Force, I believe we had the support of a parliament which understood the RAF and the threats to the UK. Furthermore, there was a mutual respect and cooperation between the United States Air Force and the Royal Air Force. With the end of the Cold War in 1991, the world changed. When I read the Strategic Defence Review launched by the Labour Government in 1997, it seemed more appropriate to 1937:

> Ability to operate offensive aircraft abroad when foreign basing may be denied.
> All required space and infrastructure; when foreign bases are available they are not always available in a conflict and infrastructure is often lacking.
> A coercive and deterrent effect when deployed to a trouble spot.

In the Labour Government from 1997 to 2010, there were six Secretaries of State for Defence and I believe three were reported as having a personal financial issues which resulted in the appointment of another Defence Secretary. Furthermore, we all know that our Prime Minister involved the UK in the Iraq War when there were no weapons of mass destruction.

On 25 July 2007 the Secretary of Defence announced that a contract had been signed to build two aircraft carriers which would be the largest ships ever to serve in the Royal Navy, at a cost of £6.2 billion. The commissioning of HMS *Queen Elizabeth* is planned for 2017 and it is expected to be operationally ready by 2020; HMS *Prince of Wales* will be launched in 2017. Currently there are no aircraft planned to operate from either carrier. Furthermore, when you examine the accuracy of pilotless drones and the monitoring of any movements around the world, the aircraft carriers would be the prime target for any enemy. As we are part of NATO, what potential enemy is likely to warrant the Royal Navy involvement with an aircraft carrier? I suggest that the purchase of two aircraft carriers is a total waste of money and emphasizes the necessity to have Secretaries of Defence who have an understanding of defence requirements, which should now be increased to study security threats. I know I repeat myself

Aerial view of Vulcan Mk2 XM645.

when I state that in 1831 the Duke of Wellington set up the Royal United Service Institute to study war, but just examine the actions of the Labour Government from 1997 to 2010. How long will we as a nation be paying for the aircraft carriers and can anyone explain their operational role? How long will they remain in service and where will they be based?

During the Second World War and the Cold War, I believe that the Western Powers, primarily the US and the UK, had politicians and military leaders who recognised the threats and fortunately made the right decisions. Following the Cold War, just examine the problems in Libya, Egypt, Sudan, Jordan, Israel, Palestine, Lebanon, Syria, Iraq, Iran, Yemen, Pakistan, Nigeria, Malaya, and North Korea.

Those who served in the V-Force dedicated their lives to preserving democracy in Western Europe while co-operating with the United States Air

V-Force: Valiant, Vulcan, and Victor on their way to Farnborough Air Display in 1958. PJG was flying the Valiant.

Force. During these years, the V-Force aircrew were the only British servicemen ever to accept the personal responsibility to drop a hydrogen bomb—a unique record in British history. I note that the government has never produced any reward to honour those who accepted this unique responsibility.

APPENDIX

Analysis of the Nuclear Capability of the Royal Air Force

CHRONOLOGY OF POLITICAL, MILITARY, AND INTERNATIONAL EVENTS

1945

May 8	German surrender
May 12	Churchill's 'Iron Curtain' speech: 'From Stettin in the Baltic to Trieste in the Adriatic, an iron curtain has descended across the continent.'
Jun 26	United Nations' Charter signed in San Francisco by fifty countries
Jul 5	General Election—Labour Party returned to power
Jul 16	First atomic device detonated at Alamogordo, New Mexico
Aug 6	Atomic bomb dropped on Hiroshima
Aug 9	Atomic bomb dropped on Nagasaki
Oct 10	Chiefs of Staff letter to Prime Minister recommending production of atomic bomb
Oct 29	Prime Minister informs House of Commons that an atomic energy research establishment is to be set up at Harwell

1946

Jan 1	Chiefs of Staff report to Prime Minister recommending a stock of atomic bombs
Jan 29	Prime Minister announces formation organisation at Risley to manufacture fissile materials
Mar 21	United States Air Force creates Strategic Air Command
May 1	UK Atomic Energy Bill published; Air Staff requirement for long range bomber circulated; SAC given responsibility for delivery of atomic weapons against an enemy
Jul 1	B-29 drops fourth atomic bomb on Bikini Atoll
Jul 25	USAF drops fifth atomic bomb—first under water crater
Aug 1	McMahon Act signed by US President setting up Atomic Energy Committee

Sep 25	UK Official Meeting on Atomic Energy holds first meeting
Oct 5	UK Government proposes to create MoD
Nov 1	Dr W. G. Penney sends proposal to MRAF Lord Portal for development of atomic weapons
Nov 6	Atomic Energy Act, 'to provide for the development of atomic energy and the control of such developments'
Nov 17	Operational requirement circulated for a medium-range bomber: speed 500 kt; height at target 45,000 feet; radius 1,500 nm

1947

Jan 8	Government decision to develop atomic bomb
Jan 24	English Electric, Handley Page, Avro and Armstrong Whitworth invited to tender for the prototype of a medium-range bomber
May	Dr Penney informed of decision to develop atomic bomb
Jul 28	Ministry of Supply decided to order the Avro design and that the Royal Aeronautical Establishment should undertake high-speed wind tunnel tests on the Handley Page crescent wing design
Oct 14	Major Charles E. Yeager, USAF, becomes first pilot to fly supersonically in a Bell X-1
Oct 19	Ministry of Supply signs contract for two Handley Page prototypes

1948

Jan	Ministry of Supply signs contact for two Vulcan prototypes
Feb 22	Communist coup d'état in Prague
Mar 4	Discussions in Brussels; Western Union Treaty between Britain, France, Belgium, Netherlands, and Luxembourg
Mar 17	Five power treaty signed in Brussels providing collective self defence
Apr 5	Collision between BEA Viking and Soviet YAK fighter over Berlin with fifteen people killed, including YAK pilot
Apr 16	Ministry of Supply signs contract for two Valiant prototypes
May 12	In answer to a parliamentary question, MoD stated that 'all types of weapons, including atomic weapons' were being developed
Jun 14	Agreed that the RAF should be trained to handle and store atomic weapons
Jun 24	Russians stop rail traffic on Berlin–Helmstedt line
Jun 25	USAF dispatches eight Dakotas to Berlin
Jun 28	A further eight Dakotas and airlift by RAF to West Berlin

July 16	Air Ministry and US Embassy in London announce that during July and August, three USAF bomber groups of thirty B-29s will be located at RAF Lakenheath, Marham, Scampton, and Waddington
Sep 3–5	Exercise 'Dagger', first UK air defence exercise since the end of the Second World War, included USAF B-29s; a military body created within the Brussels Treaty known as the Western Union Defence Organisation with headquarters at Fontainebleau
Oct 19	General Curtis Le May assumed command of SAC
Nov 9	HQ SAC opened at Offutt AFB, Omaha, Nebraska
Nov 12	Chief of the Air Staff wrote to the USAF to find out the possibility of the RAF obtaining B-29s

1949

Apr 4	North Atlantic Treaty signed in Washington between Britain, France, Belgium, Netherlands, Luxembourg, United States, Canada, Denmark, Iceland, Italy, Norway, and Portugal. Other countries joined: Greece and Turkey in 1952 and the Federal Republic of Germany in 1955
May 12	Berlin blockade lifted
May 13	First Canberra prototype flies
Jun 25–3 July	Second full scale Air Defence Exercise since the Second World War, included Western Union Air Forces
Aug 24	North Atlantic Treaty came into force
Aug 29	First nuclear explosion by Soviets near Semipalatinsk
Sep 20	Clement Attlee states, 'Research and development on atomic weapons and means of delivery are all projects to which I attach the highest importance.'

1950

Mar 22	First B-29/Washington allocated to RAF arrives in UK
Apr 1	Aldermaston taken over for atomic weapons development
Apr 10	RAF instructors complete conversion course on B-29s
Apr 13	Nos 115 and 218 Squadrons re-formed as B-29 squadrons
Apr 25	North Korean forces invade South Korea
Apr 26	United Nations Security Council orders cease fire in Korea
Apr 27	President Truman orders USAF to assist South Korea
Jul 1	US land forces committed to defence of South Korea
Sep 1	First RAF Washington Squadron formed
Sep 15	NATO Council decided that an integrated force should be created for the defence of NATO European countries and placed under a Supreme Commander
Nov 8	First F-80 *v.* Mig 15 fighter battle in Korea

Nov 15	Second RAF Washington Squadron formed
Dec	Bomber Command Jet conversion flight formed at Binbrook
Dec 18	Approval by North Atlantic Council that Germany should contribute to Western defence

1951

Jan 8	MoD order for twenty-five Valiants
Jan 27	Prime Minister reports order placed for first British four-engine jet bomber
Feb 1	Third Washington Squadron formed
Feb 9	Vickers receive order for twenty-five Valiants for delivery in 1953 at an cost of £8 million
Apr 2	General Eisenhower assumes command of Allied forces in Europe
May 18	First flight of prototype Valiant
May 25	Canberras arrive at RAF Binbrook; B-47s entered service with SAC, USAF
Aug	Bomber Command B-29 crews participated in SAC Bombing Competition
Oct 24	Russian nuclear explosion
Oct 27	Formation of Conservative Government by Winston Churchill
Dec 1	Canberra Operational Conversion Unit formed at RAF Bassingbourn

1952

Jan 12	Valiant prototype crashed and co-pilot killed
Feb	Churchill informs parliament of plans to test an atomic bomb at Monte Bello
Apr	Churchill directs the Chiefs of Staff to make a fundamental strategic review; produced Global Strategy which presented doctrine of nuclear deterrence
Apr	First flight of second Valiant prototype
May	Canberra Operational Conversion Unit opened at Bassingbourn
Jun 12	Cabinet agrees to order for fifty Vulcans
Jul 22	First Victor and Vulcan contracts and first aircraft to be delivered in 1955
Aug 30	First flight of Vulcan and appears at Farnborough Show in September
Oct 2	Air Council decides on a 'V' class of medium bombers
Oct 3	First British atomic test on Monte Bello Islands
Oct 12–18	Bomber Command Washingtons compete in SAC Bombing Competition at Davis Monthan AFB

Oct 31	First thermonuclear explosion at surface level
Nov 1	US experimental device exploded equal to 1,000 times the size of Hiroshima; Air Council agrees Handley Page aircraft will be known as Victor
Dec 4	Cutback in UK fighter production
Dec 24	First flight of Victor prototype

1953

Mar 1	Return planned of RAF Washingtons to the US
Jul 7	Return of thirty-five Washingtons to US begins
Jul 27	Armistice Agreement in Korea
Aug 1	Bomber Command Armament School formed at RAF Wittering
Aug 12	First Soviet thermonuclear detonation
Sep 3	Second prototype Vulcan (Olympus 100s) flies from Woodford
Sep 9	Assistant Chief of Air Staff describes development of Victor and Vulcan as 'very, very, slow'
Nov 7	First production model of atomic bombs delivered to RAF
Dec 8	President Eisenhower proposes to the UN General Assembly that there should be international control of atomic energy
Dec 21	First flight of production Valiant

1954

Feb 18	Statement on Defence: 'We intend, as soon as possible, to build up in the Royal Air Force, a force of medium bombers capable of using the atomic weapons to the fullest effect [...] The RAF has a major deterrent role [...] Atomic weapons are in production and delivery to the forces has begun.
Mar 1	RAF Gaydon to be first V-bomber station; US explodes thermo nuclear weapon in Marshall Islands; the test, yielding 15 megatons, was 'in a form readily adaptable for delivery by aircraft'
Mar 26	Second US thermonuclear weapon explosion
Mar 30	Prime Minister's statement in parliament about the hydrogen bomb
Mar 31	Last Washington (B-29) leaves for US
Jun 16	Cabinet Defence Committee authorises H bomb to be developed
Jun 24	Orders placed for further thirty-two Victors and thirty-two Vulcans, bringing the number for each aircraft up to fifty-seven
Jun 26	Following two Cabinet meetings, production of thermonuclear bombs authorised
Aug 3	No. 1321 Flight formed at Wittering to conduct trials on Valiant

Sep 3	Operational requirement for Blue Steel issued by Air Staff, to be in service by 1960
Nov	Ministry of Supply accepted Operational Requirement for Blue Steel
Nov 18	Air Council considers implications of setting up the Medium Bomber Force
Dec 1	Churchill informs the House of Commons that, 'the advance of the hydrogen bomb has fundamentally altered the entire problem of defence'

1955

Jan 1	No. 138 Squadron formed at RAF Gaydon
Jan 8	First Valiant B-1 flown from Wisley to Gaydon
Feb 17	Statement on Defence states that Britain is proceeding with the development and production of hydrogen bombs
Apr 1	No. 543 Squadron formed at RAF Gaydon
Apr 6	Chiefs of Staff decide to develop a weapon with a yield of 1 megaton
May 2	Orders for further fifty V-bombers approved by Cabinet Defence Committee
May 9	Formal admission of Federal Germany as a member of NATO
May 14	Warsaw Pact signed between USSR and seven Eastern European satellite states
May 26	General election and Conservatives returned
Jun 15	US–UK Agreement for Co-operation Regarding Atomic Information for Mutual Defence
Jun 29	First B-52 delivered to Castle AFB, California
Jul 4	No. 232 Operational Conversion Unit formed at RAF Gaydon for training Valiant crews
Jul 29	Valiant WP222 crashed at Wittering killing all crew
Sep 5	Two Valiants of No. 138 Squadron leave UK on proving flights to Far East
Sep 5–11	Valiants fly in SBAC Show at Farnborough
Sep 24	No. 543 Squadron formed at RAF Gaydon
Nov 6	Russian air burst nuclear explosion near Semipalatinsk
Nov 18	No. 543 Squadron at RAF Wyton—reconnaissance role
Nov 22	Largest Soviet nuclear explosion, above 1 megaton

1956

Mar 9	Development contract awarded to A. V. Roe for Blue Steel missile
Mar 16	Russian nuclear explosion with output around 40 kilotons

May 1   No. 49 Squadron at RAF Wittering to carry out nuclear trials
May 20   US air drop of thermonuclear weapon
May 31   Decided that Mk 2 version of V-bombers should be developed
Jun 19   British atomic weapons tests completed at Monte Bello Islands
Aug   Reliability trials on Vulcan at RAF Boscombe Down
Aug 15–16   RAF/USAF Meeting on co-ordination of atomic strike plans
Oct 1   Vulcan accident at London Airport on return from Australia
Oct 11   First British atomic bomb dropped at Maralinga, South
               Australia
Oct 31–Nov 6   Anglo-French operations against Egypt
Dec 12   USAF Chief of Staff writes to RAF Chief of Staff about US
               agreement in principle to supply RAF with atomic weapons in
               time of war and to co-ordinate atomic strike plans

1957
Jan 18   Vulcan Operational Conversion Unit established at RAF
               Waddington
Feb 1   US Secretary of Defence agrees to authorise discussions on the
               RAF being supplied with US atomic bombs in event of war and
               on co-ordination of USAF and RAF atomic strike plans
Mar 5 RAF and USAF discussions on co-ordination of atomic strike plans;
               Cabinet decides that additional orders should be placed for a
               force of 120 Mk 2 Victors and Valiants
Apr 4   UK Government decides not to develop supersonic bomber
May 15   First British hydrogen bomb dropped at Christmas Island
May 21   USAF/RAF Memorandum of Understanding on supply of
               atomic weapons and co-ordination of strike plans
May 21   No. 83 Squadron—first Vulcan Squadron formed at
               Waddington
May 30   Meeting of ministers agrees that Air Ministry and Ministry of
               Supply should be authorised to place order for a further forty-
               two Mk 2 V-bombers, giving a front line strength of 184
May 31   Second megaton weapon dropped on Christmas Island
Jun 19   Operation Grapple third and final test weapon dropped by No.
               49 Squadron
Aug 2   Defence Committee decides that V-Force should consist of 144
               aircraft with 104 Mk 2 versions
Sep 24   Last Valiant purchased for RAF service leaves Vickers
Oct 4   USSR launches Sputnik
Oct 6   Soviet hydrogen bomb detonated
Oct 9   Victor B-1 arrives at Boscombe Down for reliability trials
Oct 15   No. 101 Squadron formed at RAF Finningley with Vulcan Mk 1

Oct 30	Vulcans and Valiants compete in SAC Bombing Competition at Pinecastle AFB
Nov 8	Operation Grapple—second British megaton trials completed successfully
Nov 28	Victor enters service

1958

Jan	USAF operations with B-47 commenced at Greenham Common and Fairford
Feb 3	Draft Operational Requirement for extended range of Blue Steel
Feb 13	Defence White Paper states British megaton weapons in production and delivery to RAF has begun
Feb 18	Cabinet approves draft agreement with US Government on deployment of IRBMs in UK
Feb 21	1958–59 Air Estimates state that Canberras of 2nd TAF and Bomber Command will have nuclear capability
Feb 22	US–UK Agreement on installation of sixty Thor (IRBM) in eastern UK for five years; US to supply missiles and warheads, UK sites and installations
Apr 9	First Victor delivered to No. 10 Squadron, RAF Cottesmore
Apr 18	Victor Operational Training Unit established at RAF Gaydon
Apr 28	Operation Grapple—experimental megaton weapon tested at Christmas Island: dropped by Valiant of No. 49 Squadron
May 5	Canberras of 2nd TAF have been modified to carry nuclear weapons
May 15	Air Council agree to assign three Valiant squadrons (twenty-four aircraft) to SACEUR in place of Canberra force (sixty-four aircraft)
May 28	Operational requirement for extended range of Blue Steel Mk 2
Jun 11	Operational requirement for Blue Steel to have megaton warhead
Jun 21	MoD approved proposals for improving readiness of Bomber Command
Aug 29	First Western Ranger—Vulcan from Waddington, UK—Goose Bay, Labrador—Offutt AFB, Nebraska
Sep 2 & 11	No. 49 Valiant Squadron dropped nuclear devices at Christmas Island
Sep 23	Grapple megaton weapon trials completed
Nov	First Thor missiles brought to No. 77 Squadron, RAF Feltwell
Nov 18	Cabinet Defence Committee re-affirmed Medium Bomber Force as 144 aircraft
Dec 17	Secretary of State for Air announced decision to develop a new strike/reconnaissance aircraft to replace the Canberra

1959

Jan	Vickers and English Electric chosen as main contractors to develop TSR-2, the Canberra replacement
Jan 22	Joint USAF/RAF requirement for 1,000 nm range missile
Apr 16	First launch of Thor missile by RAF crew at Vandenburg AFB
May 8	Operational requirement for TSR-2 issued
May 20	Air Marshal K. B. B. Cross appointed C-in-C of Bomber Command, replacing Air Chief Marshal Sir H. Broadhurst
Jul 9	Valiant flown by Wg Cdr M. J. Beetham makes first non-stop flight to Cape Town in 11 hours and 52 minutes and flight refuelled twice
Jul 27	Minister of Defence asks for six-monthly reports on state of readiness of Bomber Command
Aug 20	Prototype Victor Mk 2 lost over Irish Sea; when wreckage recovered cause was loss of pitot tube
Oct 14	General Election in United Kingdom Ministry of Aviation formed
Oct 28	First successful Valiant–Vulcan flight refuelling
Dec 31	Assignment of first Valiant squadron to SACEUR

1960

Jan 1	Blue Steel Mk 2 cancelled
Feb 17	Government White Paper says that the Ballistic Missile Early Warning Station will be at Fylingdales in Yorkshire and is the third in the system with Alaska and Greenland
Mar 2	Secretary of State for Air says the RAF could get four V-bombers airborne from one airfield in less than four minutes
Mar 29	First French atomic explosion in Sahara
Mar 29	Agreement between US President and UK Prime Minister to co-operate in development and acquisition of Skybolt
May 1	U-2 shot down over Soviet Union
May 25–26	Valiant makes first non-stop flight to Singapore refuelled twice by Valiant tanker
Jun 3	HQ Task Force Grapple disbanded
Jun 6	Understanding on Skybolt between US and UK
Jun 18	British Aircraft Corporation formed
Jul 1	First Vulcan B-2 delivered to RAF Waddington
Jul 25	Chief of Defence Staff cancels twenty-five of fifty-seven Victor B-2s on order
Jul 27	First Blue Steel flown
Jul 31	End of campaign against communist terrorists in Malaya
Aug	Nos 617 and 44 Squadrons formed Vulcan B-1

Sep 5–12	Scramble by four Valiants, Victors, and Vulcans at SBAC Display
Sep 12–20	First Anglo-American conference on Skybolt held in US
Sep 15	Canberras in Germany placed on QRA
Sep 27	Technical agreement on Skybolt between US Department of Aviation and UK Ministry of Aviation
Oct 7	Minister of Defence places full development contract for TSR-2
Dec 15	Confirmed order for fifty-seven Blue Steel missiles; US informs UK that Skybolt order being slowed

1961

Jan 29	Forty-four Thor missiles take part in Exercise Respond
Mar 9–10	First flight-refuelled flight by Vulcan from UK to Nairobi
Jun 20–21	Vulcan 1A flew non-stop from RAF Waddington to Sydney, Australia; first non-stop UK-Australia—flight-refuelled by Valiant tankers—11,500 miles in 20 hours 3 minutes
Jul 1	RAF Hunter ground attack aircraft and troops sent to Kuwait following request of ruler; Valiants at Malta on readiness
Jul 13	V-bombers Mk 2 to be given simultaneous engine starting
Aug 13	Berlin Wall begun
Sep 1	No. 617 Squadron equipped with Vulcan B-2
Sep 11	Disbandment of last Bomber Command Canberra squadron
Oct 14	Exercise Skyshield—Vulcans participate for the first time in US national air defence exercise; four from Nos 27 and 83 Squadrons
Nov	Victor B-2 introduced into operational service
Dec 5	Micky Finn—first Bomber Command readiness exercise without prior notice

1962

Jan 1	Beginning of QRA commitment in Bomber Command; one aircraft per squadron on 15 minutes readiness; Medium Bomber Force readiness brought in line with Valiants under SACEUR
Feb 1	First Victor B-2 brought into squadron service in No. 139 Squadron at RAF Wittering
Feb 15	USAF/RAF Skybolt trials with Vulcan at Eglin AFB
Apr 19	First live launch of Skybolt 'partially successful'
Jun 29	Second 'hot' launch of Skybolt from B-52 failed to ignite
Jul	Agreement that there should be initial purchase of 100 Skybolt missiles and 90 warheads
Jul 3	Successful air launching of Blue Steel at Woomera range
Jul 9	Cabinet decided that 100 Skybolts should be ordered

Aug 1	Joint US/UK agreement that deployment of Thor IRBMs to UK would be ended in 1963
Aug 4	No. 617 Squadron equipped with Blue Steel
Sep 20–22	Bomber Command Readiness Exercise Micky Finn; 101 out of 112 available aircraft and 59 out of 60 Thor missiles
Nov 22	Air Council confirm that Victors 1/1A should replace the Valiant in the tanker role
Dec 18–21	Kennedy and Macmillan talks in Bermuda; President's decision to cancel Skybolt

1963

Jan 2	Defence Research Policy Committee endorsed development of laydown bomb to allow V-bombers to operate at low level
Jan 23	Cabinet Defence Committee agrees proposals to allow V-bombers to operate at low level and to development of high yield laydown bomb
Jan 31	Whole of V-bomber force assigned to NATO but independent use not restricted
Feb 14	C-in-C Bomber Command stated that Blue Steel was in service and that Bomber Command had 23,216 personnel of whom 10,620 were in the V-Force
May 23	RAF V-Force formally assigned to NATO for targeting, planning, co-ordination and execution of strikes
May 31	Canberra QRA in Germany increased from four to eight
Aug 15	RAF Thor Force non-operational
Aug 25	'No notice' alert exercise initiated by AOC in O Bomber Command
Aug 28	Blue Steel cleared for use by Vulcans on QRA
Sep 17	Flylingdales Ballistic Missile Early Warning Station declared operational
Sep 27	Last Thor missile returned to the USA
Oct 1	Defence Research Policy Committee supports proposal for Blue Steel to be modified to operate at low level
Nov 19	Successful trials to launch Blue Steel at low level
Dec	No. 139 Squadron Victor B-2 based at Wittering converted to Blue Steel; operations in Malaya and Borneo against Indonesian confrontation
Dec 31	Run-down of Thor Force completed

1964

Feb 4	Secretary of State for Air confirms that the V-Force equipped and trained to attack from low level

Jun 30	RAF Christmas Island closed
Aug 6	Inspection reveals rear spar in Valiant fractured
Aug 10	Final low-level release of Blue Steel from Victor at Woomera
Sep 27	TSR-2 makes first flight
Oct	Change of government—Labour Administration
Oct 26–29	Exercise Micky Finn—Bomber Command no-notice dispersal exercise to test alert and readiness
Dec 9	Valiants grounded except for national emergency
Dec 31	TSR-2 makes second flight

1965

Jan 25	SACEUR informed that Valiants being withdrawn from service due to fatigue failure
Apr 3	No. 380 Bomb Wing returned to US after nearly twelve years of operations at RAF Brize Norton
Apr 6	Chancellor of Exchequer, James Callagham, announces cancellation of TSR-2 project
Apr 7	Practice reinforcement of Far East by eight Vulcans
May 1	Victor B(K).1 Tanker Force now based at RAF Marham; No. 543 Squadron at RAF Wyton equipped with Victor Mk 1
Jun 30	HQ 7th Air Division, SAC, discontinued
Jul 1	Control of RAF Gaydon transferred to Flying Training Command; order for 158 General Dynamics terrain-following radar for Victor Mk 2 and Vulcan Mk 2
Dec 14	500th 'Western Ranger' Flight to Offutt AFB, Nebraska

1966

Jan	No. 543 Squadron, Wyton, now Victor Mk 2
Feb 22	Fifty F-111s ordered from United States
Aug 11	Malaysia–Indonesian Treaty signed in Bangkok
Aug 16	Withdrawal of USAF units from France
Sep 1	Three Victor squadrons to be re-formed as three-point tankers
Dec 8	Bomber Command making changes for nuclear attacks 'from high level to low level'

1967

May 3	Evacuation of Aden
May 31	First Vulcan launch of Blue Steel
Jun	Arab Israeli six-day war
Jul 7	Second Vulcan Blue Steel firing
Dec	No. 101 Squadron re-equipped with Vulcan Mk 2

1968

Jan 16	F-111A project cancelled
Jan	No. 44 Squadron re-equipped with Vulcan Mk 2
Apr 1	Strike Command formed, amalgamating Fighter and Bomber Commands
Sep 30	No. 100 Squadron—Victor 2s—disbanded
Dec 31	No. 139 Squadron—Victor 2s—disbanded

1969

Jan	Operational Requirement Committee agreed that Victor Mk 2 should replace present aircraft in tanker force
Jun 30	Medium Bomber Force QRA terminated
Jul 1	UK based V-bombers transferred to tactical role
Jul 28	Exercise High Noon (no notice alert and readiness exercise replacing Micky Finn) held first time since QRA ended for Vulcans
Aug	No. 83 Squadron disbanded
Aug	Plan to convert twenty-four Blue Steel Vulcans to free fall
Nov	Following withdrawal of Blue Steel by end of year, whole Vulcan force to use low-level free fall nuclear weapons—WE-177B

RAF SQUADRONS INVOLVED IN THE NUCLEAR DETERRENT

With the development of jet engines and the introduction of nuclear weapons after the Second World War, the role of the Royal Air Force changed. In 1970 it changed again with the development of nuclear-powered submarines with the capability of firing nuclear missiles. When the Tornados entered service they also had a nuclear role. The responsibilities of the RAF are detailed by squadron.

No. 7 Squadron

1956	Nov	Valiant squadron formed at RAF Honington
1961		Relocated to RAF Wittering
1962	Oct	Squadron Disbanded

No. 9 Squadron

1962	Mar	Vulcan B-2 squadron formed at RAF Coningsby
1964	Nov	Relocated to RAF Cottesmore
1966		WE-177 laydown nuclear weapon assigned to SACEUR
1969–74		Based at RAF Akrotiri in Cyprus; UKs commitment to CENTO

1975–82		Based at RAF Waddington; WE-177 laydown nuclear weapon; assigned to SACEUR
1982	Apr	Disbanded
1982	Aug	First Tornado GR1 squadron at RAF Honington; WE-177 laydown nuclear weapon assigned to SACEUR
1986		RAF Bruggen, Germany
1994		End of nuclear role
1999		First Tornado GR4 squadron
2001	Jun 15	Ended continuous RAF presence in Germany since Second World War
2001	Jul 17	RAF Marham

No. 10 Squadron

1958	May	Victor B-1 squadron reformed at RAF Cottesmore
1964	Feb	Disbanded

No. 12 Squadron

1962	Aug	Vulcan B-2 squadron Reformed at RAF Coningsby
1967	Dec	Disbanded

No. 15 Squadron

1958	Sep	Victor B-1 squadron formed at RAF Cottesmore
1964	Oct	Disbanded

No. 27 Squadron

1961	Apr	Reformed at RAF Scampton with Vulcan B-2 fitted with Blue Steel
1969	Jul	Vulcan B-2 squadron fitted with WE-177B laydown weapon of 450-kt yield; assigned to SACEUR for low-level penetration
1971		Disbanded
1973	Dec	Vulcan B-2 reformed at RAF Scampton in Maritime Radar Reconnaissance role and assigned to SACEUR
1982		Vulcan B-2 squadron disbanded
1983		Reformed at RAF Marham with Tornado GR1 and WE-177 laydown nuclear weapon; assigned to SACEUR
1993		Tornado squadron disbanded

No. 35 Squadron

1962	Dec	Vulcan B-2 squadron reformed at RAF Coningsby
1964	Nov	Vulcan B-2 squadron relocated to RAF Cottesmore
1966		WE-177 laydown nuclear weapons assigned to SACEUR

1969–74		Based at RAF Akrotiri in Cyprus; UK's commitment to CENTO; WE-177 laydown nuclear weapon
1975–82		Based at RAF Scampton; WE-177 laydown nuclear weapon; assigned to SACEUR
1982	Mar	Disbanded

No. 44 Squadron

1960	Aug	Vulcan B-1 reformed at RAF Waddington
1968		Vulcan B-2; WE-177 laydown nuclear weapons; assigned to SACEUR
1969		Vulcan B-2 fitted with WE-177B laydown nuclear weapon of 450-kt yield; assigned to SACEUR for low-level penetration
1982	Dec	Vulcan B-2 squadron disbanded

No. 49 Squadron

1956	May	Valiant squadron formed at RAF Wittering
1956	Oct 11	First Air Drop of an atomic bomb
1957	May 15	Dropped atomic bomb of 1 megaton; Valiant XD818 in RAF Museum at Cosford
1957	Nov 8	Operation Grapple—atomic bomb yield 1.8 megatons
1958	Apr 28	Operation Grapple—atomic bomb yield 3.0 megatons
1958	Sep 23	Operation Grapple—Balloon drop 25 kilotons; last nuclear weapon dropped by the UK
1965	May	Disbanded

No. 50 Squadron

1961	Aug	Vulcan B-1 squadron reformed at RAF Waddington
1966	Jan	Reformed with Vulcan B-2 fitted with WE-177B laydown bomb; assigned to SACEUR for low-level penetration
1982	Jun	Six aircraft converted for tanker role
1984	Mar	Disbanded

No. 55 Squadron

1960	Sep	Victor B-1A squadron reformed at RAF Honington
1965	May	Relocated to RAF Marham for tanker conversion
	Aug	Operational tanker squadron
1982		Tanker support during Falklands War
1991		Deployed to Gulf as part of Operation Granby, invasion of Kuwait
1993	Oct	Nos 55 and 57 Squadrons—last Victor squadrons to be disbanded

No. 57 Squadron

1959	Jan	Victor B-1 squadron reformed at RAF Honington
1965	Nov	Reformed at RAF Marham as a tanker squadron
1982		Tanker support during Falklands War
1991		Deployed to Gulf as part of Operation Granby, invasion of Kuwait
1993	Oct	Nos 55 and 57 Squadrons—last Victor squadrons to be disbanded

No. 83 Squadron

1957	May	Vulcan B-1 formed at RAF Waddington
1960	Oct	Reformed at RAF Scampton with Vulcan B-2
1969	Aug	Squadron disbanded

No. 90 Squadron

1957	Jan	Valiant squadron formed at RAF Honington
1961	Aug	Part refuelling role
1962	Apr	Tanker squadron
1965	Apr	Squadron disbanded

No. 100 Squadron

| 1962 | May | Victor B-2 squadron formed at RAF Wittering |
| 1968 | Sep | Squadron disbanded |

No. 101 Squadron

1957	Oct	Vulcan B-1 formed at RAF Finningley
1961	Jun	Relocated to RAF Waddington
1967	Oct	Reformed with Vulcan B-2; Vulcan B-2 fitted with WE-177B laydown bomb of 450-kt yield; assigned to SACEUR for low-level penetration
1982	Aug 4	Squadron disbanded

No. 138 Squadron

1955	Feb	First Valiant squadron formed at RAF Gaydon
1955	May	Relocated to RAF Wittering
1962	Apr	Squadron disbanded

No. 139 Squadron

| 1962 | Feb | Victor B-2 squadron formed at RAF Wittering |
| 1968 | Dec | Squadron disbanded |

No. 207 Squadron

| 1956 | Apr | Valiant squadron formed at RAF Marham |
| 1965 | May | Disbanded |

No. 214 Squadron

1956	Mar	Formed at Marham as Valiant squadron
1965	Feb	Disbanded as Valiant squadron
1966	Jul	Formed at RAF Marham as Victor tanker squadron
1977	Jan	Victor B-2 squadron disbanded

No. 543 Squadron

1956	Mar	Formed at Gaydon as a Valiant Photographic Reconnaissance Squadron
1956	Nov	Reformed at RAF Wyton
1964	Dec	Valiant squadron disbanded
1965	May	Reformed as a Victor B-1 Reconnaissance Squadron
1966	Jan	Reformed as Victor B-2 Reconnaissance Squadron
1970	Mar	Relocated to RAF Honington
1970	Oct	Returned to RAF Wyton
1974	May	Victor squadron disbanded

No. 617 Squadron

1958	Aug	Reformed as Vulcan B-1/1A squadron at RAF Scampton
1961	Sep	Vulcan B-2
1962	Aug	Vulcan B-2 Blue Steel
1970	Jan	Vulcan B-2 fitted with WE-177B laydown bomb of 450-kt yield; assigned to SACEUR for low-level penetration
1981	Dec	Disbanded
1983	Jan	Reformed at RAF Marham with Tornado GR1 with WE-177 laydown bomb until 1994